GRADE
5
AGES 10-11

SCORE!
Mountain Challenge

**LANGUAGE ARTS
WORKBOOK**

KAPLAN

PUBLISHING
New York

This publication is designed to provide accurate and authoritative information in regard to the subject matter covered. It is sold with the understanding that the publisher is not engaged in rendering legal, accounting, or other professional service. If legal advice or other expert assistance is required, the services of a competent professional should be sought.

Contributing Editor: Justin Serrano
Editorial Director: Jennifer Farthing
Editorial Development Manager: Tonya Lobato
Assistant Editor: Eric Titner
Production Editor: Dominique Polfliet
Production Artist: Creative Pages, Inc.
Cover Designer: Carly Schnur

Published by Kaplan Publishing, a division of Kaplan, Inc.
888 Seventh Ave.
New York, NY 10106

Printed in the United States of America

May 2007
10 9 8 7 6 5 4 3 2 1

ISBN-13: 978-1-4195-9463-2
ISBN-10: 1-4195-9463-X

Kaplan Publishing books are available at special quantity discounts to use for sales promotions, employee premiums, or educational purposes. Please email our Special Sales Department to order or for more information at kaplanpublishing@kaplan.com, or write to Kaplan Publishing, 888 Seventh Avenue, 22nd Floor, New York, NY 10106.

Table of Contents

How to Use Your *SCORE! Mountain*
Challenge Workbook . . . . **iv**

Time to Get Organized and
Learn to Use Your Time Wisely! . . . . **vii**

SCORE! Mountain Challenge
Online Instructions . . . . **xii**

Base Camp 1: Vocabulary **1**

Base Camp 2: Writing Structure **29**

Base Camp 3: Grammar and Mechanics **57**

Base Camp 4: Reading Nonfiction **85**

Base Camp 5: Reading Fiction **119**

Base Camp 6: Everyday Writing **155**

Tools **187**

Are you ready for a fun and challenging trip up *SCORE!* Mountain?

Getting Started

This exciting, interactive workbook will guide you through 6 unique base camps as you make your way up *SCORE!* Mountain. Along the way to the top, you will have the opportunity to challenge yourself with over 150 language arts questions, activities, and brain busters as you work toward conquering *SCORE!* Mountain.

To help you figure out the answer to each question, use the blank space on the page or the extra pages at the back of your workbook. If you need extra space, use a piece of scrap paper.

Base Camp

SCORE! Mountain is divided into 6 base camps—each covering an essential language arts topic—and is aligned to the educational standards set forth by the National Council of Teachers of English. The final base camp in this workbook, Everyday Writing, has a special focus on the many ways we might use writing each day.

Your trip through base camp will take you through 19 questions related to the base camp topic, a Challenge Activity designed to give your brain an extra workout, and a 5-question test to see how much you've learned during your climb.

Each question comes with helpful hints to guide you to the right answer. Use these hints to make your climb up *SCORE!* Mountain a successful learning experience!

The Answer Hider

We encourage you to give each question your best effort before looking at the answer; that's why your *SCORE! Mountain Challenge Workbook* comes equipped with a handy answer hider.

Tear out the answer hider and while you work on each question, use your answer hider to cover up the solution until you're finished. Then uncover the answer and see how well you did!

Celebrate!

At the end of each base camp, there's a fun celebration as a reward for successfully making it through. It's the perfect opportunity to take a break and refresh yourself before tackling the next base camp!

SCORE! Mountain Challenge Online Companion

Don't forget—more fun awaits you online! Each base camp comes with a set of 10 online questions and interactive activities, plus a mountain-climbing study partner who will encourage you and help you track your progress as you get closer to the top of *SCORE!* Mountain!

SCORE! online base camps are designed to supplement the educational themes of each base camp from the workbook. As you reach the end of each base camp in the workbook, we encourage you to go to your computer to round out your *SCORE!* Mountain Challenge experience. Plus, after you successfully complete the last online base camp, you are awarded a Certificate of Achievement.

Certificate of Achievement

Upon completion of the entire workbook and online program, you will receive your very own Certificate of Achievement that can be shared with family and friends!

Time Management

In addition to all of the great language arts practice that your *SCORE! Mountain Challenge Workbook* has to offer, you'll find an array of helpful tips and strategies at the front of the workbook on how you can best organize and manage your time to stay on top of your busy schedule, do well at school, get all of your homework and chores done, and still have time for fun, family, and friends! It's a great way to help you perform at your best every day!

Tools

Every mountain climber needs a set of tools to help him or her reach the mountaintop! Your *SCORE! Mountain Challenge Workbook* has a special set of tools for you. In the back of your workbook you'll find a handy guide to help you get through each base camp. Turn to the back of the workbook and use these tools whenever you need a helping hand during your climb up *SCORE!* Mountain.

Enjoy your trip up *SCORE!* Mountain. We hope that it's a fun and educational learning experience!

GOOD LUCK!

Being organized and managing your time well are very important skills to learn. It's a valuable key to success!

Here are some tips to help.

Getting Started

- *Be realistic.* We all wish that we had an endless number of hours in the day to take care of all of our responsibilities and still have time for all of the fun things we want to do. The truth is that every person in the world has the same amount of time to work with. Each of us gets 24 hours a day, 7 days a week, so how you budget your time is important!

- *Keep a schedule.* To help you keep track of your time, try creating a weekly schedule. You can use a calendar or organizer, or you can make your own schedule on a blank piece of paper. Your weekly schedule might look like this:

My Weekly Schedule

	MON.	TUES.	WED.	THURS.	FRI.	SAT.	SUN.
6:00 A.M.							
7:00 A.M.							
8:00 A.M.							
9:00 A.M.							
10:00 A.M.							
11:00 A.M.							
12:00 P.M.							
1:00 P.M.							
2:00 P.M.							
3:00 P.M.							
4:00 P.M.							
5:00 P.M.							
6:00 P.M.							
7:00 P.M.							
8:00 P.M.							
9:00 P.M.							
10:00 P.M.							

- *Budget time.* Set aside time on your schedule for all of your regular daily activities. For instance, if you go to school between 7:00 A.M. and 2:30 P.M. each weekday, write that on your schedule. Be sure to include any important chores, responsibilities, after-school clubs, and special events. Budget time for homework and school assignments as well, but also make time for fun with your friends and family!

Staying Organized

- *Write it down.* The best way to keep track of new activities or assignments is to write them down. Whenever something new comes up, add it to your schedule!

  You can also try keeping a "To Do" list to make sure you remember everything. Try to estimate the amount of time it will take to complete your assignments. It's a good way to budget your time!

- *Have a daily plan.* Each day, plan out what chores, assignments, and activities you have to do that day. Use your "To Do" list to help. Some activities may take up more time, so make sure you have enough time that day to complete everything. Your daily plan might look something like this:

Sample Daily Plan

MONDAY	
6:00 A.M.	Get up, get dressed
7:00 A.M.	Eat breakfast Go to school
7:40 A.M.	School starts
2:30 P.M.	School ends Karate Club meeting – gym
3:30 P.M.	Get home from school
4:00 P.M.	Homework and chores (see "To Do" list)
6:30 P.M.	Dinner
7:30 P.M.	Call friends and watch TV
8:45 P.M.	Get ready for bed
9:00 P.M.	Bed

Doing Homework

- *Set homework time*. Your schedule should include a block of time for doing homework. If possible, make this block of time for right after school is finished, so you're sure to have enough time to complete your assignments. How much time do you usually need for homework? Write that on your weekly schedule.

- *Get right to it!* When it's time to do your homework, stay focused. Try to work straight through until you get it done. You'll be happy to finish, so you can move on to other fun things! Sometimes a small, healthful snack can help keep you going and energized!

- *Stay organized*. Set up your homework space in a well-lit area with all the things you'll need to do a great job. This includes your schoolbooks, a dictionary, a calculator, pens, and extra paper. If you keep these items handy, it makes learning a lot more organized and fun!

- *Improve your skills*. Good students develop their skills both inside and outside the classroom. Your *SCORE! Mountain Challenge Workbook* can help. Set aside part of your homework time each day for completing sections from the workbook. Check your progress with the online quizzes as well.

Chores and Activities

- *Keep your commitments*. Remember to include your chores in your daily schedule. You might even set aside a "chore time." Be sure to include chores on your daily "To Do" list as well.

- *Know your limits*. How many school activities can you manage? Be realistic when you join clubs or sign up for activities. Activities are fun, but you must make time for all of the other things going on in your life.

- *Set priorities*. If you don't have many commitments, you can get everything done in your free time. But what if you're committed to more things than you have time for? Then you must set priorities.

  A **priority** is something that's important to you. When you set priorities, you choose the items from your list that are most important to complete.

Use the worksheet below to help you determine your priorities.

Priorities Worksheet

Review the list of activities below. Write your own activities in the blank spaces next to Clubs, Sports, and Classes. Add any other activities on the lines next to Other.

In the column marked Priority, give each activity a letter: **A**, **B**, or **C**:

- **Priority A** = very important to me
- **Priority B** = important to me
- **Priority C** = less important to me

Priority	Activity	Priority	Activity
_____	Homework _____	_____	Sports _____
	_____	_____	_____
_____	Chores _____	_____	Other _____
_____	_____	_____	_____
_____	Clubs _____	_____	_____
_____	_____	_____	_____
_____	Classes _____	_____	_____
_____	_____	_____	_____

List your top 5 priorities below. These items are the most important to you. You should always focus on getting these done.

Priority	Activity
1	
2	
3	
4	
5	

Once you know what's important to you, make sure the things that are top priority get done first!

Setting Goals

- Even though you're busy, it's also great to try new things Setting goals will help you with this!

- Maybe you want to try a new sport, join a new club at school, or read a new book? Fill in the spaces below to help you get started reaching your goals. Every time you reach a goal, make a new goal for yourself. You'll be amazed at how much you can do!

What is your #1 goal?

_____

_____

How are you going to reach your #1 goal?

_____

_____

Leaving Time for Fun!

- Everyone needs time to relax and recharge. Include some time in your schedule for relaxing and just having fun with your family and friends. You'll be glad you did!

Your *SCORE! Mountain Challenge Workbook* comes with a fun, interactive online companion. Parents, go online to register your child at **kaptest.com/scorebooksonline**. Here your child can access 60 exciting language arts activities and a cool mountain-climbing study partner.

Children, when you log on, you'll be brought to a page where you will find your *SCORE! Mountain Challenge Workbook* cover. You'll also be asked for a **password**, which you will get from a passage in this workbook. So have your workbook handy when you're ready to continue your *SCORE!* Mountain Challenge online, and follow the directions.

Good luck and have fun climbing!

Base Camp

1

Vocabulary

Are you ready to begin climbing *SCORE!* Mountain? Let's get started! Good luck!

SCORE! MOUNTAIN TOP

BASE CAMP 5

BASE CAMP 4

BASE CAMP 3

BASE CAMP 2

BASE CAMP 1

1. Choose the word that is closest in meaning to the word *circulated*, as used in the following sentence:

   Blood is *circulated* throughout the body by the pumping of the heart.

   Ⓐ created

   Ⓑ increased

   Ⓒ lost

   Ⓓ moved

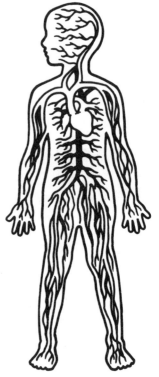

Hint #1:

Many words contain the Latin root *circum-*, which means **around.** You can remember this by thinking of a circle!

Hint #2:

When your heart is pumping, what does that do to your blood?

Answer: Choice **D** is correct.

Circulated is closest in meaning to the word **moved**. *Circulate* means to **move along a path and then return to the same place**, as the blood moves around the body. *Circulate* also means **to move from person to person** or **from place to place**, for example, a person who moves from group to group at a party is **circulating**.

2. Choose the word that is closest in meaning to the word *pending*, as used in the following sentence:

> Beth wasn't sure if she would be allowed to go to the mall with her friends; her mom's decision was still *pending*.

(A) difficult

(B) nice

(C) undecided

(D) unfair

Hint #1:

The Latin root *pend-* means **hang** or **hanging**. Think of Beth's mom's decision as "hanging" to help you to find the closest synonym.

Hint #2:

You can also use **context clues** to help you to find the answer. Beth is still waiting to see if she will be allowed to go, so which choice makes the most sense?

Answer: Choice **C** is correct.

Beth's mom's decision is still **hanging**, which means **not yet decided**. The root *pend-* also shows up in words like *dependent*, meaning **relying or hanging onto someone or something for support**, or *suspend,* meaning **to cause to hang**. You can also use the **context clues** to help you; because Beth is still waiting for an answer from her mom, it makes the most sense that her mom is still **undecided**.

3. Which of these words probably comes from the Latin root *mar-*, meaning **"belonging to the sea"**?

Ⓐ marshal

Ⓑ marina

Ⓒ Martian

Ⓓ oceanic

Hint #1:

Remember, the word you are looking for must meet two conditions; it must be related to the Latin root *mar-*, and its meaning must have to do with the **sea** or **ocean**.

Hint #2:

Have you ever used the words in the answer choices? How have you used them?

Answer: Choice **B** is correct.

A *marina* is **a place for docking boats**, and it comes from the Latin root *mar-*.

4. Choose the word that most likely comes from the Latin word *terra*, meaning "**land**."

(A) territory

(B) terrible

(C) term

(D) plot

Hint #1:

Think about which one of these words names a **kind of land**, an **amount of land**, or a **specific piece of land**.

Hint #2:

Remember to use your reading and writing experience! Have you ever read or used these words before? How have you used them or seen them used?

Answer: Choice **A** is correct.

A *territory* is a **large area of land**, or **land belonging to someone**, and comes from the Latin word *terra*.

5. Choose the word that is closest in meaning to the word *grazed*, as used in the following sentence:

The cattle *grazed* in the fields.

Ⓐ ran
Ⓑ ate
Ⓒ fought
Ⓓ lazed

Hint #1:

Eliminate choices that seem too extreme.

Hint #2:

Use **context clues** to help you to find the answer.

Answer: Choice **B** is correct.

Grazed is a **synonym** for *ate*. When answering synonym or antonym questions, be sure to eliminate choices that are far-fetched or that you know do not make sense.

6. Choose the word that is **closest** in meaning to the word *tale*, as used in the following sentence:

Wendy told us a sad *tale* about a boy who lost his puppy.

(A) story

(B) chase

(C) event

(D) mouse

Hint #1:

Try each answer choice in place of the word *tale*. Which one would make the most sense inserted in the sentence?

Hint #2:

Remember to search for context clues to help you figure out the meaning of the word!

Answer: Choice **A** is correct.

The best **synonym** for *tale* is *story*. Try it out in the sentence, in place of *tale*. It still has the same meaning, doesn't it?

7. Choose the word that is **closest** in meaning to the word *remain*, as used in the following sentence:

Jenna plans to *remain* in town until after the holidays.

(A) stay

(B) go

(C) live

(D) leave

Hint #1:

Think about which word makes the most sense in the sentence.

Hint #2:

Eliminate the answer choices that don't fit in the sentence!

Answer: Choice **A** is correct.

The best **synonym** for *remain* is *stay*.

8. Choose the word that is the **same** or **nearly the same** as the underlined word.

      Inform the public.

  (A) force

  (B) anger

  (C) tell

  (D) crowd

Hint #1:

Think about ways you might have heard the word *inform* being used.

Hint #2:

Have you ever used the word *inform* in something you have written? If so, how did you use it?

Answer: Choice **C** is correct.

To *inform* means **to give information**, or **to tell.**

Read the passage carefully, then answer questions 9 and 10.

Aardvarks are African mammals. They feast on bugs, including ants and termites. Aardvarks have <u>sharp</u> hearing, which is useful when they are catching prey. They have <u>sleek</u>, dark fur, long ears, and strong claws that look like hooves.

9. Choose the word that means the **opposite** or **nearly the opposite** of the underlined word *sharp* as used in the passage.

Ⓐ weak

Ⓑ dull

Ⓒ flat

Ⓓ round

Hint #1:

Think of how the word *sharp* is used in the passage.

Hint #2:

Make sure you read the question carefully to be sure you understand what it is asking you to find.

Answer: Choice **A** is correct.

The word *weak* is the best **antonym** for *sharp* as it's used in the passage. In this passage, *sharp* means **strong**, and *weak* has the **opposite** meaning. Thinking about the meaning of the word in the passage and then predicting an opposite will really help you to eliminate the tempting but wrong answer choices.

10. Choose the word that means the **opposite** or **nearly the opposite** of the word *sleek* as used in the passage.

Ⓐ shiny

Ⓑ dull

Ⓒ fat

Ⓓ slow

Hint #1:

Think about how *sleek* is being used in the passage.

Hint #2:

Try and make a **prediction** about what the answer is **before** you look at the answer choices. This makes it easier to narrow them down and find the correct one!

Answer: Choice **B** is correct.

The word *dull* is the best **antonym** for *sleek*.
In the passage, *sleek* means **glossy** and **shiny**, which is the **opposite** of *dull*.

© Kaplan Publishing, Inc.

11. Choose the word that means the **opposite** or **nearly the opposite** of the underlined word below.

The **rapid** pace of the cars

Ⓐ slow

Ⓑ steady

Ⓒ large

Ⓓ fast

Hint #1:

Think about how you've heard the word used before, and then make a **prediction** about the answer. Do any of the answer choices match your prediction?

Hint #2:

Are you looking for a **synonym** or **antonym**? Be careful!

Answer: Choice **A** is correct.

The word *rapid* means **fast**, so the best **opposite** is *slow*.

12. Choose the word that is most nearly the **opposite** of the word *drowsy*.

（A）pretty

（B）skillful

（C）sleepy

（D）awake

Hint #1:

Because the question doesn't give you any **clues**, think about how you've heard this word used before. Then, make a **prediction**.

Hint #2:

Eliminate the choices that you know aren't correct.

Answer: Choice **D** is correct.

The word *drowsy* means **sleepy**, so the best opposite is *awake*.

13. In which answer choice does the word *work* have the **same meaning** as in the sentence below?

The students take great pride in their *work*.

Ⓐ The light switch doesn't *work*.

Ⓑ Jeff had to *work* on Friday.

Ⓒ Harry realized that his plan wasn't going to *work*.

Ⓓ "Did you finish your *work*?" asked Julie's mom.

Hint #1:

A good first step would be to think about what **part of speech** the word *work* is in each sentence.

Hint #2:

Think about the definition of *work* as it is used in the sentence and choose the answer choice that most closely matches.

Answer: Choice **D** is correct.
The word *work*, as used in the sentence, is a **noun**. In choice **D**, "*'Did you finish your work?' asked Julie's mom*," *work* is also used as a **noun**. In the other answer choices, it's used as a **verb**.

14. Choose the word that **best** completes the sentence.

"I don't think Dad will let us go to the party," said Matthew, "you know he can be very _____ when it comes to going to sleepovers on school nights."

(A) relaxed

(B) silly

(C) straightforward

(D) rigid

Hint #1:

Use the first part of the sentence to help you to determine which word will work best in the blank.

Hint #2:

How does Matthew's dad feel about having sleepovers on school nights?

Answer: Choice **D** is correct.

The word that **best** completes the sentence is *rigid*.

Rigid means **strict** or **tough**. Matthew thinks that his dad will not let them go on a sleepover on a school night, so the only word that makes sense here is *rigid*.

15. Choose the word that **best** completes the sentence.

Firefighters are _____ with proper gear to protect them as they work.

Ⓐ happy
Ⓑ strong
Ⓒ equipped
Ⓓ chased

Hint #1:

First, eliminate choices that don't make sense in the sentence. That way, even if you don't know all of the words, you'll have fewer to choose from.

Hint #2:

Remember, try to guess what a good word to complete the sentence would be, and then look through the answer choices for the word that most closely matches your guess.

Answer: Choice **C** is correct.

Because the sentence is telling about firefighters' gear, the best word to complete the sentence is **equipped**, which means **supplied with tools**.

16. Choose the word that correctly completes **both** sentences.

At the end of the high-speed _____ , two of the cars smashed together.

The dog always tries to _____ the cat, but he can never catch her.

(A) catch

(B) chase

(C) crash

(D) fight

Hint #1:

Be sure to go back and reread both sentences with your choice inserted in the blank to be sure it makes sense.

Hint #2:

If an answer choice fits in one sentence but **not** the other, then eliminate it!

Answer: Choice **B** is correct.

The only choice that properly completes both sentences is *chase*.
In the first sentence, *chase* is being used as a **noun**. In the second sentence, *chase* is being used as a **verb**.

17. Choose the **best suffix** to fill in the blank in the sentence.

I moved all of the heavy **box**___ by myself.

(A) -es

(B) -s

(C) -ed

(D) -ing

Hint #1:

Often, it helps to **write out** the word with each of the endings in the answer choices added to see which ending looks correct.

Hint #2:

Eliminate the choices that do not fit in the blank.

Answer: Choice **A** is correct.

The sentence should read: **I moved all of the heavy box̲e̲s̲ by myself.** We add the suffix **-es** to words that end in **-x** or **-s** to make them **plural.** The proper way to pluralize **box** is **boxes.**

18. Pick the answer choice that provides the **best** definition for the **underlined prefixes** below.

<u>re</u>read   <u>re</u>join

(A) hard

(B) stop

(C) again

(D) first

Hint #1:

What does **read** mean? What does **reread** mean?

Hint #2:

What does **join** mean? What does **rejoin** mean?

Answer: Choice **C** is correct.

Reread or **rejoin** means to **read** or to **join again**. The meaning of the prefix **re-** is **again**.

19. Choose the answer that provides the **best definition** for the **underlined suffixes** below.

    window<u>less</u>   fear<u>less</u>

(A) clear

(B) containing

(C) afraid

(D) without

Hint #1:

Be sure to pay close attention to what the question is asking!

Hint #2:

Watch out for tempting answer choices that are synonyms or have similar meanings to the given words.

Answer: Choice **D** is correct.

To be **windowless** or **fearless** means to be **without windows** or **without fear.** The best meaning of the suffix **-less** is **without.** Pay close attention to what the question is asking; it's only asking about the **meaning** of **-less**, **not** about the **meanings** of the **words.**

© Kaplan Publishing, Inc.

Challenge Activity

You're doing a great job so far!
Are you ready for a Challenge Activity?

Good luck!

a) Match each word below to its definition.

_____ **pendulum**   A. The distance around a figure, area, or object

_____ **terrarium**   B. One who works on or navigates a ship

_____ **mariner**   C. A hanging device used to keep time in clocks

_____ **circumference** D. A small enclosure for plants or animals

b) Write a **synonym** for the word below:

comprehensive

synonym: _____

c) Write an **antonym** for the word below:

stagnant

antonym: _____

See hints and answers on following page.

Think about the definitions of the **word roots** in the previous activities.

Think about how you have used these words or have seen them used before.

Answers to Challenge Activity:

a) **pendulum—C**
A *pendulum* is **a hanging device used to keep time in clocks**.
Pendulum has the Latin root *pend-*, which means **hanging**.

terrarium—D
A *terrarium* is **a small enclosure for plants or animals**.
Terrarium has the Latin word *terra*, which means **earth**.

mariner—B
A *mariner* is **one who works on or navigates a ship**.
Mariner has the Latin root *mar-*, which means **ocean** or **sea**.

circumference—A
Circumference is **the distance around a figure, area, or object**.
Circumference has the Latin root *circum-*, which means **around**.

b) There are many synonyms for the word *comprehensive*.
Here's an example:
synonym: **complete**

Did you come up with this synonym or a different one?

c) There are many antonyms for the word *stagnant*.
Here's an example:
antonym: **active**

Did you come up with this antonym or a different one?

Test

Let's take a quick test and see how much you've learned during this climb up *SCORE!* Mountain.

Good luck!

1. Choose the word that means the opposite or nearly the opposite of the underlined word in the sentence below.

   Harry's <u>durable</u> sneakers lasted much longer than Mary's; hers fell apart after only a week.

   Ⓐ long lasting

   Ⓑ small

   Ⓒ athletic

   Ⓓ delicate

2. Choose the best definition for the underlined word below.

   The teacher asked Billy to <u>revise</u> his work for the third time.

   Ⓐ grade himself

   Ⓑ hand in on time

   Ⓒ look over to improve

   Ⓓ put away

3. Choose the word that is the closest synonym of the underlined word below.

<u>Motionless</u> water

(A) still

(B) clear

(C) silent

(D) choppy

4. Choose the word that is the closest antonym of the underlined word below.

Marjorie and Allison had an unpleasant <u>dispute</u> about whose turn it was to feed the puppy.

(A) agreement

(B) argument

(C) discussion

(D) bet

5. Choose the one word that best completes both sentences below.

Brandy pushed a _____ hair out of her face.

Our cat isn't allowed to _____ too far out of the yard.

(A) loose

(B) wander

(C) walk

(D) stray

Answers to test questions:

1. Choice **D** is correct.
   The word *durable* means **long lasting**, or **sturdy**. You can find clues about the meaning of *durable* in the sentence. Because the sentence is telling us that Harry's shoes lasted **much longer** than Mary's, *durable* must have something to do with **lasting a long time**, or **not falling apart easily**.

2. Choice **C** is correct.
   Revise means to **look over to improve**. The prefix *re-* means **again**, and the Latin root *vis-* means having to do with **looking** or **seeing**. To *revise* work means to look it over for the purpose of improving it.

3. Choice **A** is correct.
   The suffix *-less* means **without**. *Motionless* water means water **without motion**, or water that is **still**.

4. Choice **A** is correct.
   A *dispute* is an **argument** or a **disagreement**. If you didn't know the meaning of the word *dispute*, using **context clues** would have been a good strategy. The adjective *unpleasant* is a clue that the girls were not working very well together to take care of the puppy!

5. Choice **D** is correct.
   The word *stray*, when used as an **adjective**, means **escaped** or **out of place**, which works in the **first sentence**. The word *stray*, when used as a **verb**, means **to wander away**, which works in the **second sentence**. Be sure to read the words in each sentence and think about whether they make sense in both.

Celebrate!

Let's take a fun break before we go to the next base camp. You've earned it!

Let's make a family tree!

Making your family tree is a lot of fun, and a great way to learn more about your family and yourself!

Directions:

- Start with the basic outline of a family tree:

Congratulations! You're on your way to the top of *SCORE!* Mountain.

- Each person on your family tree is a **tree limb**, connected to the immediate members of his or her family.

- It's easiest to start with **yourself** and work your way **backward**.

- Connect yourself to your brothers and sisters if you have any.

- Then connect you and them to your parents.

- Connect your parents to their brothers and sisters (they are your aunts and uncles).

- Add in the children of your aunts and uncles (they are your cousins).

- Connect your parents, aunts, and uncles to your grandparents.

- You can continue tracing your family history as long as you like. The farther you go, the bigger your tree will be!

- Ask your parents or a relative for help if you're not sure of all the members of your family.

- You can decorate your family tree any way you'd like! Some ideas are adding fun colors and photos of your relatives.

- When you're finished, share your family tree with your family members!

Good luck and have fun!
You deserve it for working so hard!

Base Camp

2

Writing Structure

Let's continue to climb up *SCORE!* Mountain. Are you ready? Let's get started! Good luck!

1. Which choice below is a **correct** and completely
written sentence?

(A) David to park with Julian and Mandy the other day.

(B) Sitting in the first row, Nick could observe all of the
actors closely.

(C) Singing silently and humming to herself walking along
the street.

(D) The three of us skipping along happily.

Hint #1:

Be sure the answer you choose
has **both** a **subject** and a **verb**,
the two parts of a complete
sentence.

Hint #2:

Eliminate the answer choices
that don't seem like correct and
complete sentences. It may
help to say each answer choice
out loud.

Answer: Choice **B** is correct.

The **subject** of the sentence is *Nick* because *Nick* is whom the sentence is
about. The **verb phrase** is *could observe*. None of the other choices have
both a **subject** and a **verb** that tells about the subject or tells what the
subject is doing.

2. Choose the answer that is **not** a complete and correctly written sentence.

(A) The three girls, Nancy, Taryn, and Caroline, are afraid of scary movies.

(B) Can you possibly guess what happened to me last night?

(C) Sadly, the girl wept and wept.

(D) Once upon a time in the lovely village of Lancaster.

Hint #1:

First, try to determine the **subject,** whom or what each sentence is about.

Hint #2:

Next, find the **verb** that either tells what the subject did or that links the subject with some information about the subject.

Answer: Choice **D** is correct.

Choice **D** is the only group of words that is **not** a **complete sentence**. In this case, *once* is the **subject**. The phrases *upon a time* and *in the lovely village of Lancaster* are **prepositional phrases** that describe *once*. There is **no verb** that tells about *once*. The other choices all contain a **subject** and **verb**.

Read the letter below and answer question 3.

> Dear Greg,
>
> My trip to Brazil has been wonderful. Yesterday, we went to visit the rainforest. We seen many amazing animals!
>
> Your friend,
>
> Chris

3. What is the **best** way to write **sentence 3**?

(A) We see many amazing animals!

(B) We are seeing many amazing animals!

(C) We saw many amazing animals!

(D) We have seen many amazing animals!

Hint #1:

Think about whether the letter is in **past**, **present**, or **future tense**.

Hint #2:

Sometimes it helps to say a sentence out loud to determine if it is correct or not.

Answer: Choice **C** is correct.

The letter is written in the **past tense**, so choice **C**, **We saw many amazing animals**, is correct. Choice **D** is also in past tense, but *have seen* would only work if Chris was talking about seeing the animals **over a long period of time**. Because he is only talking about **one time**, *saw* is the best choice.

4. Which answer choice shows the **best** way to write the sentence?

  (A) Out in the freezing cold, John left his skateboard.

  (B) John and his skateboard left out in the freezing cold.

  (C) John in the freezing cold left his skateboard.

  (D) John left his skateboard in the freezing cold.

Hint #1:

Think about the thought that is being expressed in the answer choices. Which choice **best** expresses this thought?

Hint #2:

How would you tell someone what happened? Look for the choice that most closely matches what you would say.

Answer: Choice **D** is correct.

Choice **D** is the **best choice** because it is clearly written and makes the most sense.

5. The following sentences are part of a paragraph. Which of the sentences would be the best **topic sentence** of that paragraph?

Ⓐ Often, knights would create poems and songs about the fair lady.

Ⓑ During the age of Chivalry, knights had to follow a strict code of conduct.

Ⓒ One of the rules of the code was that knights had to protect women and children, and knights would often choose a special lady and fight in her honor.

Ⓓ Knights were also required to treat prisoners fairly and respectfully.

Hint #1:

Think about what all the sentences together are about—that's your **topic**.

Hint #2:

Look for the sentence that **introduces** the paragraph topic or **best explains** what all of the other sentences are about.

Answer: Choice **B** is correct.

All of the sentences are about **the age of Chivalry. Chivalry** is a code of conduct, or a way of behaving, that all knights had to follow in the Middle Ages. Choice **B** is the one that **introduces the topic**. The other sentences give **examples** of rules that the knights followed and **ways** that they acted during this time period.

© Kaplan Publishing, Inc.

6. The following incomplete paragraph is **missing a topic sentence.** Read the paragraph carefully, then choose the **best** topic sentence to complete the paragraph.

When we go camping, the first thing we do is check our campsite to be sure that it is free of poisonous plants and beehives. Then, my dad begins to put up the tent, and my mom and I gather branches to make a fire. When my mom and I make the fire, we are very careful that everything is cleared out of the way and that no one is nearby. We always bring a first aid kit with us in case someone gets hurt while we are hiking. When we leave the campsite, we make sure that we didn't leave anything behind and that the fire is put out completely so it will not spread. Because we are such careful campers, we always have a wonderful time!

- (A) My family takes safety very seriously on camping trips.
- (B) Camping is only fun if you can make a huge fire.
- (C) My family enjoys going camping.
- (D) My favorite camping trip was last year in the Rocky Mountains.

Hint #1:

Be sure the topic sentence you choose represents what the **whole** paragraph is about.

Hint #2:

Remember to look for the sentence that introduces the paragraph topic or best explains what all of the other sentences are about.

Answer: Choice **A** is correct.

The paragraph is about the speaker's family **taking safety precautions when going on camping trips**, so choice **A** is the best topic sentence.

7. The following **incomplete paragraph** is **missing a topic sentence**. Read the sentences carefully. Then, choose the **best topic** sentence to complete the paragraph.

Jake is a black cat, but his fur is starting to turn white because he is getting old. However, Jake is very smart. He comes when I call him, and he also knows how to play hide and go seek. Jake is also very polite. He never tries to eat people food; he only eats his own food. Jake is the best pet I've ever owned, and I hope he lives to be 100!

(A) Cats are so much fun to have around.

(B) My favorite pet is my cat, Jake.

(C) Even though he is hard work, Jake is a good cat.

(D) It is very important to train cats properly from a young age.

Hint #1:

Consider what the paragraph is **mainly about**, and read the concluding sentence carefully.

Hint #2:

Remember to look for the sentence that introduces the paragraph topic or best explains what all of the other sentences are about.

Answer: Choice **B** is correct.

The writer of this paragraph is **describing** her cat Jake and talking about why she believes that Jake is such a good pet. Remember, the concluding sentence can give us a **good clue** about the topic of the paragraph, and here the writer tells us that the speaker thinks that **Jake is the best pet she has ever owned**. Choice **B** best expresses the main idea.

8. The following sentences are in **scrambled order.** When they are unscrambled, they make up a **paragraph.**

Choose the **best order** for the sentences.

1. The tops of the temples were painted red as a gift to the gods.

2. They were made out of limestone, which is still used in buildings today.

3. Although they look nothing like they did during the Classic Age, it is truly amazing to witness these incredible works of art.

4. During the Classic Age of the Mayans, people created huge pyramids for their kings and their gods.

5. These temples were constructed carefully, with specific colors and building materials.

Ⓐ 5, 1, 3, 4, 2

Ⓑ 4, 5, 1, 2, 3

Ⓒ 4, 1, 2, 3, 5

Ⓓ 3, 4, 5, 1, 2

Hint #1:

First, find the topic sentence, or the sentence that introduces the topic for the first time.

Hint #2:

Eliminate all of the choices that do not list the topic sentence first.

Answer: Choice **B** is correct.

Sentence 4 is the best **topic sentence**, and should be first, because it tells that the paragraph is about the temples that the Mayans built during the Classic Age. **Sentence 5** tell us that the pyramids were constructed carefully, with specific materials, and **sentences 1** and **2** give more information about the temples, that they were built with limestone and painted red, so they should follow **sentence 5**. **Sentence 3** is the **best concluding sentence** because it summarizes what the paragraph is about.

Read the following sentences, then answer question 9.

1. Then, spread peanut butter on one side.

2. First, lightly toast two pieces of fresh bread.

3. Place the jellied piece on top of the other piece, cut the bread in half, and enjoy!

4. Next, spread the jelly on the other piece of bread.

5. There are many ways to make a peanut butter and jelly sandwich, but, in my opinion, there is one way that is better than all the others.

9. Which of the following is the **best order** for the sentences?

   Ⓐ 5, 2, 1, 4, 3

   Ⓑ 1, 2, 4, 5, 3

   Ⓒ 2, 1, 4, 3, 5

   Ⓓ 5, 2, 4, 1, 3

Hint #1:

Find the best topic sentence, and then think about the order of events in the paragraph.

Hint #2:

Remember, the **topic sentence** appears **first** in the paragraph, and the **concluding sentence** appears **last**.

Answer: Choice **A** is correct.

The **best topic sentence** in this case is **sentence 5** because it tells us that the paragraph is going to be about making a peanut butter and jelly sandwich. The first step is toasting the bread, so **sentence 2** is next. Then, we lightly spread the peanut butter, **sentence 1**. Next, we spread the jelly on the other piece of bread, **sentence 4**. Finally, **sentence 3** is the **concluding sentence**. We know it's the concluding sentence because at the end it says "*enjoy*," which tells us the sandwich is finally ready to eat!

10. The following paragraph is **missing a sentence**.
Read the paragraph and the missing sentence that follows.
Then, choose the **best** place for the sentence.

(1) Soccer fans are some of the most extreme sports fans in the world. (2) One example of this dangerous behavior happened at a game in the Stadio Olimpico in Central America. (3) Two local teams were playing each other in a very important game. (4) When one team scored a goal, the other team's fans got so angry, they set the stadium on fire! (5) No other sport in the world has such rowdy and excitable fans.

Missing sentence: Soccer fans have been known to get so excited during games that they do things that are slightly crazy, and even downright dangerous.

Where is the **best** place for the missing sentence?

(A) after sentence **(5)**

(B) before sentence **(1)**

(C) after sentence **(1)**

(D) before sentence **(4)**

Hint #1:

When reading the paragraph, look for **transitions** between sentences that are confusing or awkward.

Hint #2:

You can try placing the missing sentence where each answer choice suggests. Which place does the missing sentence fit best?

Answer: Choice **C** is correct.

The transition between **sentences 1** and **2** is confusing. **Sentence 2** gives an example of this dangerous behavior, but **sentence 1** doesn't say anything about danger. Adding the missing sentence **after sentence 1** makes the paragraph much clearer.

11. Susan is writing an **essay** about her trip to Cozumel, Mexico. Which of the following is the best **hook** for her introductory paragraph?

Ⓐ On my trip to Mexico, I was snorkeling peacefully, when suddenly I saw a huge barracuda up ahead.

Ⓑ Cozumel is a city in eastern Mexico.

Ⓒ Mexico can be a fun place to visit.

Ⓓ Have you ever been to Europe?

Hint #1:

A good **hook** is a beginning sentence that draws the reader's interest and makes him or her want to read on.

Hint #2:

Think about which sentence most makes you want to continue reading.

© Kaplan Publishing, Inc.

Answer: Choice **A** is correct.

Susan should start with a surprising story related to her trip to draw the reader in and make the beginning of her essay interesting. Choice A is the best **hook sentence**.

12. Which of the following sentences **least** belongs in Susan's **introductory paragraph**?

(A) Cozumel is one of the best vacation spots in the world.

(B) The Mayan ruins are about a fifteen-minute drive from the beach.

(C) In addition to snorkeling, Cozumel is also an amazing vacation spot because there are beautiful Mayan ruins there and the food is excellent.

(D) Great snorkeling is just one of the many reasons why Cozumel is a wonderful place to visit.

Hint #1:

The **introductory paragraph** should "**hook**" the reader's interest.

Hint #2:

Another function of the introductory paragraph is to introduce the **supporting points** you will make in your essay.

Answer: Choice **B** is correct.

Choice **B** is a **detail** that belongs in Susan's paragraph about the Mayan ruins, but least belongs in her introduction. **Sentence A** states Susan's **thesis**, or main idea, and belongs in the introduction. **Sentence C** states Susan's **main points**, which are reasons that Cozumel is one of the best vacation spots. **Sentence D** is a good transition between the **hook** and the **main points**.

13. **Now you try it!** Write your own **hook sentence** for Susan's introductory paragraph.

Write your sentence on the lines below.

_____

_____

_____

_____

Hint #1:

Remember, a good hook is a beginning sentence that draws the reader's interest and makes him or her want to read on.

Hint #2:

Remember what Susan's essay is about!

Answer: Everyone's hook sentence will be different, but here are a few **guidelines** to follow:

Think about whether your hook sentence is **interesting** and **will draw the reader in**. Did you use a question, a quote, or a surprising story? Here is an example, using a question to hook the reader:

Have you ever dreamed of getting away to white beaches, sun, and crystal blue water?

Your hook sentence may be different, and that's fine, as long as you follow the guidelines to writing a good hook sentence!

14. Which of the following would **not** be a good **topic sentence** for one of Susan's **body paragraphs**?

Ⓐ Snorkeling is one of Cozumel's main attractions, and it is a very fun activity.

Ⓑ The Mayan ruins in Cozumel provide an example of the city's rich history.

Ⓒ One of the most enjoyable times of the day in Cozumel is mealtime.

Ⓓ Renting a ski boat is also a very fun activity to do in Cozumel.

Hint #1:

Review Susan's three main points in question 12.

Hint #2:

Think about the key elements of a good topic sentence.

Answer: Choice **D** is correct.

Ski boats are **not** mentioned as one of Susan's main points in her introduction, so choice **D** would **not** make a good topic sentence.

15. Match the following **detail sentences** to the **body paragraph topic sentences** that they belong with by placing the letter of the body paragraph topic sentences in the appropriate blank.

Detail Sentences:

_____ 1. The ruins date back to the Pre-Classic Period of the Mayan Civilization, approximately 600 C.E.

_____ 2. My absolute favorite Mexican dish is called *chile con carne*.

_____ 3. Some people who need glasses have snorkeling gear with magnification so that they can see the fish better.

Body Paragraph Topic Sentences:

A. Snorkeling is one of Cozumel's main attractions, and it is a very fun activity.

B. The Mayan ruins in Cozumel provide an example of the city's rich history.

C. One of the most enjoyable times of the day in Cozumel is mealtime.

Hint #1:

Be sure the detail sentence provides a **detail** about the body paragraph topic sentence.

Hint #2:

Use each body paragraph topic sentence only once.

© Kaplan Publishing, Inc.

Answer: 1. B   2. C   3. A

Sentence 1 supports **topic sentence B**, because it is about the Mayan ruins.

Sentence 2 is about the food, so it supports **topic sentence C**.

Sentence 3 supports **topic sentence A**, because it is about snorkeling.

16. Now you try it! Write a sentence that belongs in each of Susan's body paragraphs.

A. Snorkeling is one of Cozumel's main attractions, and it is a very fun activity.

_____

_____

_____

_____

B. The Mayan ruins in Cozumel provide an example of the city's rich history.

_____

_____

_____

_____

C. One of the most enjoyable times of the day in Cozumel is mealtime.

_____

_____

_____

_____

Hint:

Be sure your sentences **support**, or provide **more information** about, Susan's topic sentences.

Answer: Everyone's detail sentences will be different because everyone writes differently!

Be sure that your detail sentences are only about the **topic sentences**, not about other parts of the essay.

Here are some examples:

A. A great place to rent snorkeling gear is at Bernie's Snorkel Shack.

B. One of the most beautiful structures in the ruins is a huge pyramid that used to be painted red.

C. We tried almost every restaurant in town on our trip.

17. Susan is working on her **concluding paragraph**. Which of the following **best** restates Susan's thesis for her **concluding paragraph**?

Ⓐ There are many excellent vacation spots in the world.

Ⓑ Mexico has fun and enjoyable activities for the entire family.

Ⓒ One time, we took a trip to Cozumel, Mexico.

Ⓓ Although I've been on many fun vacations with my family, undoubtedly our vacation to Cozumel, Mexico, was the best.

Hint #1:

In the **concluding paragraph**, you should restate your thesis.

Hint #2:

Go back to review the thesis sentence from **question 12**. Think about which sentence best restates this sentence.

Answer: Choice **D** is correct.

Choice **D** best restates Susan's thesis for her concluding paragraph.

The thesis statement from question 12 is: **Cozumel is one of the best vacation spots in the world.** We can eliminate choice **A** because it doesn't mention Cozumel at all. Choice **B** doesn't do the best job of restating Susan's thesis, so it can be eliminated as well. Choice **C** does not belong in the conclusion because Susan has already stated that her family took a trip to Cozumel, so we can eliminate that. Choice **D** does the best job of restating Susan's thesis.

18. Which of the following would **best** place Susan's paper in a **larger context**, by making a suggestion for an outcome or a consequence?

(A) Because of Cozumel's many wonderful tourist attractions, I predict that it will become a very popular vacation spot over the next ten years.

(B) I think that eventually people will stop coming to Cozumel.

(C) I think my class will like snorkeling.

(D) The descendants of the Mayans are planning to build a bigger museum to hold artifacts from the ruins.

Hint #1:

Remember that the points in the conclusion should be about the essay as a whole.

Hint #2:

Eliminate any answer choices that are too specific or unrelated to Susan's paper.

© Kaplan Publishing, Inc.

Answer: Choice **A** is correct.

Choice **A** does a good job of placing the paper in a larger context because Susan loved her trip to Cozumel, and she predicts that others will love Cozumel, too.

19. Now you try it! Write a different sentence for Susan's conclusion that places the paper in a larger context by relating it to life or the real world.

_____

_____

_____

_____

_____

_____

_____

_____

Hint #1:

Be sure your sentence is related to Susan's thesis statement.

Hint #2:

Be sure that your sentence is general enough to be about Susan's entire essay, but specific enough that it narrows in on her thesis.

Answer: Everyone will have a different sentence.

As long as your sentence is related to Susan's thesis statement, and is general enough to be about Susan's entire essay but specific enough that it narrows in on her thesis, then you're on the right track!

Challenge Activity

You're doing a great job so far!
Are you ready for a Challenge Activity?

Good luck!

Let's put all of your essay writing knowledge to good use!

An **essay topic** is provided for you below. On a few separate sheets of paper, **follow the outline below** and **write your own essay**!

Here is the essay topic:

My Favorite Book

I. Introduction

    a) Hook sentence
    b) Thesis sentence
    c) 3 supporting reasons or points

II. Body Paragraph 1

    a) Topic sentence 1
    b) 3 detail sentences

III. Body Paragraph 2

    a) Topic sentence 2
    b) 3 detail sentences

IV. Body Paragraph 3

    a) Topic sentence 3
    b) 3 detail sentences

V. Concluding Paragraph

    a) Restate thesis
    b) Summary of points
    c) Place essay in larger context

Answers to Challenge Activity: Everyone's essay will be different. As long as you follow the rules of good essay writing, you're on the right track!

Let's take a quick test and see how much you've learned during this climb up *SCORE!* Mountain.

Good luck!

1. Which answer choice is the best sentence?

   (A) Flies, at the beach our lunch are attacking.

   (B) Flies, attacking our lunch at the beach.

   (C) Flies are attacking our lunch at the beach.

   (D) At the beach, flies our lunch are attacking.

2. Which of the following is a complete sentence?

   (A) Trying out the game, the boys in the park.

   (B) Going to the park and walking quickly.

   (C) Michael and I to the park.

   (D) Jack quickly beat me at tennis.

3. Choose the best order for the following sentences.

   1. The plants then convert the sunlight, water, and carbon dioxide into a simple sugar called glucose.

   2. Have you ever wondered what plants eat?

   3. Plants make food through a process called photosynthesis.

   4. The plants use the glucose for food, and they release oxygen and water into the atmosphere as waste products.

   5. Plants take in sunlight and carbon dioxide through their leaves, and water through their roots.

   (A) 1, 2, 3, 4, 5

   (B) 2, 3, 5, 1, 4

   (C) 3, 5, 1, 4, 2

   (D) 2, 1, 4, 5, 3

4. Which of the following sentences in the paragraph in question 3 is the topic sentence?

(A) sentence 1

(B) sentence 2

(C) sentence 3

(D) sentence 4

5. Choose the best topic sentence for the following group of sentences.

One of the first "sightings" is recorded as taking place in the sixth century. Saint Columba, who was trying to convert people to Christianity, supposedly tamed the wild beast in Loch Ness and stopped her from killing people. In modern times, there have been many people claiming to have seen Nessie. In 1934, a doctor claimed to have photographed Nessie while on an expedition to the lake. Many people were very excited about the photo, but scientists proved that it was a fake. Many others throughout history have claimed to have seen the monster, and several other fake photographs have been produced. However, so far, Nessie has not been proven to exist.

(A) People throughout history have believed many far-fetched myths and legends.

(B) The Loch Ness monster lives in Scotland.

(C) Nessie, the monster that supposedly lives in Loch Ness in Scotland, has been the subject of many questionable sightings.

(D) Fake photographs are difficult to produce, but are also difficult to disprove.

Answers to test questions:

1. Choice **C** is correct.

   The sentence "***Flies are attacking our lunch at the beach***" is best because it is written clearly and the words are in the correct order. It is clear who or what is the **subject** of the sentence, ***flies***, and what they are doing, ***attacking***.

2. Choice **D** is correct.

   The sentence "***Jack quickly beat me at tennis***" is a **complete sentence** with a **subject** and a **verb**.

3. Choice **B** is correct.

   Sentence 2 should go first. It is a good **hook sentence** for this paragraph, because it is a question that draws the reader in and gets him or her interested. The other sentences describe the process of photosynthesis, so they should be in the order that things happen in photosynthesis, which is correct in choice **B**. The final sentence in the paragraph, **sentence 4**, is the **last step** in the process.

4. Choice **C** is correct.

   The topic sentence is **not** always the first sentence in a paragraph. **Sentence 2**, the first sentence, is a **hook sentence**, which draws the reader in. **The topic sentence**, which is the sentence that best describes what the paragraph is about, is **sentence 3**, because the topic of the paragraph is the process of photosynthesis.

5. Choice **C** is correct.

   This paragraph is about the **Loch Ness monster**, so the correct topic sentence should mention her, which choice **C** does.

Celebrate!

Let's take a fun break before we go to the next base camp. You've earned it!

Let's make a **pen pal**!

Having a pen pal is a lot of fun, and it's a great way to learn about how boys and girls live different lives all around the world!

Congratulations!
You're getting closer to the top of *SCORE!* Mountain.

Here are some tips on getting started:

- Pick a city or country that you want to have a pen pal in.
  Have you ever wanted to learn about a certain city or country and how people there live?

- Next, ask a teacher or an adult to help you find a school in that city or country.

- Then, write a letter to the school, telling the people there who you are and that you'd like to find a pen pal in their school.

- Ask your teacher if you can use your school's address on your letter, or ask your parents or guardian for permission to use your own address.

- Finally, send off your letter. I hope that you will get a response and a great new pen pal!

- Trade letters with your new pen pal. Get to know your new friend and what it's like to live where he or she lives!

Good luck and have fun!

You deserve it for working so hard!

Base Camp

3

Grammar and Mechanics

Are you ready for another fun climb up *SCORE!* Mountain? Let's get started! Good luck!

SCORE! MOUNTAIN TOP

BASE CAMP 5

BASE CAMP 4

BASE CAMP 3

BASE CAMP 2

BASE CAMP 1

1. Choose the **underlined** part of the following sentence that contains a **punctuation** or **capitalization error**.

"Lorelei, Ryan, and Benny love going to the park,
Ⓐ   Ⓑ   Ⓒ

said Benny's mother.
Ⓓ

Hint #1:

Think about the proper way to punctuate speech.

Hint #2:

Think about the types of words that should and should not be capitalized.

Answer: Choice **C** is correct.

In this sentence, Benny's mother says, **"Lorelei, Ryan, and Benny love going to the park."** There should be **quotation marks** both **before** and **after** what she says, so **quotation marks** are needed after the comma in choice **C**.

2. What type of sentence is the following?

Do you want to order the frog legs, the trout, or the liver?

(A) declarative

(B) exclamatory

(C) interrogative

(D) compound

Hint #1:

Some sentence types express the **purpose** of the sentence.

Hint #2:

Think about the **action verb** that is similar to each sentence type. Is this sentence being used to **declare** something, to **exclaim** something, or to **interrogate**?

Answer: Choice **C** is correct.

This is an **interrogative sentence**, which is a sentence whose **main purpose is to ask a question**. Think of the verb *interrogate*, which means **to question**.

3. Choose the sentence below that contains a **capitalization error**.

(A) I went to see *Gone with the wind* with my friend Annie.

(B) Annie's mother loves to watch that movie over and over.

(C) Annie and her brother Charles have seen *The Wind in the Willows* many times.

(D) This Friday, I will go with them to watch it again.

Hint #1:

Compare the answer choices that have **similar phrases** but **different capitalization**.

Hint #2:

What types of words and phrases are **always** capitalized?

Answer: Choice **A** is correct.

The main words in **titles** must be capitalized. *Wind*, in the movie title *Gone with the Wind*, should be capitalized.

Refer to the following passage to answer questions 4 and 5.

This <u>Friday,</u> <u>march</u> 1st, marks the second <u>anniversary</u> of my
     1   2   3

<u>Town's</u> annual Red <u>Ribbon</u> Festival. The <u>festival</u> always
  4   5   6

begins with the <u>Mayor</u> posing for a picture with our local
                7

<u>celebrity,</u> Odie <u>Remuflemeyer.</u> Then, the parade begins in
   8   9

the <u>North</u> end of town and finishes at <u>Northwood</u> <u>bank.</u>
    10   11   12

4. Which of the following underlined words in the passage contains a **capitalization error**?

(A) 1

(B) 2

(C) 5

(D) 8

Hint #1:

Some nouns are **always** capitalized.

Hint #2:

Some nouns are only capitalized in certain circumstances.

Answer: Choice **B** is correct.

March should be capitalized when it is the name of a month. The names of the months and the days of the week are always capitalized.

5. Which of the following underlined words does **not** contain a **capitalization error**?

     Ⓐ 4

     Ⓑ 5

     Ⓒ 10

     Ⓓ 12

Hint #1:

Be sure to read the question carefully! Only one of the answer choices does **not** contain an error.

Hint #2:

Remember the correct rules of capitalization!

Answer: Choice **B** is correct.

Only choice **B**, *Ribbon* does not contain an error. **Ribbon** should be capitalized in this case because it is part of the festival's title.

Read the following sentence, then answer questions 6 and 7.

How old will you be one week from today, on $\underset{1}{\underline{\text{Friday}}}$ May $\underset{2}{\underline{14}}$

6. What **punctuation mark** should be placed after **word 1**?

Ⓐ   ?

Ⓑ   !

Ⓒ   :

Ⓓ   ,

Hint #1:

Reading a sentence aloud often gives you **clues** as to how it should be punctuated.

Hint #2:

Try each answer choice in the sentence. Eliminate any choices that do not fit.

Answer: Choice **D** is correct.

A **comma** should be placed between the day of the week and the month when writing a date. Saying the sentence aloud can help you properly punctuate the sentence, because commas usually go where we naturally take a pause when speaking.

7. What **punctuation mark** should be placed after word 2 in the sentence?

(A))

(B) ?

(C) .

(D) !

Hint #1:

Think about what **type** of sentence this is, and how it should be punctuated.

Hint #2:

Remember, sometimes it helps to try each answer choice in the sentence. Eliminate any choices that do not fit.

Answer: Choice **B** is correct.

A **question mark** should go after number 2. Because this is an **interrogative sentence**—a sentence that asks a question—it should be punctuated with a question mark at the end.

Read the following sentence, then answer questions
8 and 9.

I drank a tall cold lemonade Harry had some iced tea
      1   2
and lemon.

8. What is the best way to **punctuate** the words in **underlined phrase 1**?

   Ⓐ drank, a tall cold

   Ⓑ drank a tall cold,

   Ⓒ drank a tall, cold

   Ⓓ drank a tall, cold,

Hint #1:

Think about how to separate two adjectives.

Hint #2:

Remember, reading the sentence aloud can often be helpful if you're not sure of the correct answer.

Answer: Choice **C** is correct.

In **underlined phrase 1**, the only place a comma is needed is between the two adjectives. When a noun has two or more adjectives that are describing it and they can be placed in either order, a comma is used to separate them. There is no need to add a comma to any other part of this phrase.

9. What is the **best** way to punctuate the words in **underlined phrase 2**?

(A) lemonade, Harry had

(B) lemonade, "Harry had

(C) lemonade: Harry had

(D) lemonade; Harry had

Hint #1:

Think about the sentence **as a whole**, not just the group of words that are underlined.

Hint #2:

Remember, if you're not sure, reading the sentence aloud can often be helpful.

Answer: Choice **D** is correct.

A **semicolon** should be placed between *lemonade* and *Harry*. A **semicolon** should be placed between two independent clauses that are not joined by a conjunction, such as **and, or**, or **but**.

10. The following sentence is **missing a punctuation mark**.

"I have no idea what you're talking about, growled Andrew, rolling his eyes.

Choose the **punctuation mark** that is missing in the sentence.

(A) "

(B) ;

(C) ,

(D) .

Hint #1:

Read the sentence carefully. What is happening in the sentence? This should give you a clue as to which punctuation mark is missing.

Hint #2:

For this question, you do not have to know exactly where missing punctuation should be placed, just what is missing.

Answer: Choice **A** is correct.

Quotation marks should be placed on either side of speech. In this case, the second set of quotation marks belongs after the comma after the word **about**, to show that Andrew has finished speaking.

The sentence should be written as follows: **"I have no idea what you're talking about," growled Andrew, rolling his eyes.**

11. Choose the sentence that is **punctuated correctly**.

Ⓐ My favorite song, by far, is "This Land Is Your Land" by Woody Guthrie.

Ⓑ My favorite song by far is This Land Is Your Land by Woody Guthrie.

Ⓒ My favorite song, by far is, This Land Is Your Land by Woody Guthrie.

Ⓓ My favorite song by far is "This Land Is Your Land" by Woody Guthrie

Ⓔ My "favorite song" by far is This Land Is Your Land! by Woody Guthrie.

Hint #1:

One strategy is to focus on one part of the sentence. Decide which is the correct punctuation for that part, and then eliminate the other choices.

Hint #2:

What can you do when you need a clue as to whether or not a sentence is correct? Say it aloud!

Answer: Choice **A** is correct.

Names of songs, poems, short stories, and articles should be punctuated with **quotation marks**.

12. Which of the following sentences is **written correctly**?

    Ⓐ A fine flock of birds fly over my house every year.

    Ⓑ My dad, my mom, and I am sitting on the front porch.

    Ⓒ The boy and his dad gathers up twigs to make a fire.

    Ⓓ Sometimes Lily and I like to swing on the swing set.

Hint #1:

Be sure the **verb** agrees with the subject in number and person.

Hint #2:

It is often tempting to make the verb agree with the word that comes before it and not with the subject, so be careful!

Answer: Choice **D** is correct.

Choice **D** is the only sentence that does **not** have an error in subject/verb agreement. When writing sentences that contain a phrase between the subject and the verb, it is often tempting to make the verb agree with the word that comes before it and **not** with the subject. For example, in choice **A,** the subject is **flock**, which is **singular**, **not plural**, so the **verb** should also be in **singular** form. The correct form of the verb in this case is **flies**.

13. Which of the following sentences is written correctly?

(A) Esmay, Matthew, and Nikhil are going to the baseball game to see Matthew's brother has played.

(B) Esmay, Matthew, and Nikhil is going to the baseball game to see Matthew's brother playing.

(C) Esmay, Matthew, and Nikhil are going to the baseball game to see Matthew's brother play.

(D) Esmay, Matthew and Nikhil are going to the baseball game to see Matthew's brother plays.

Hint #1:

Be sure the **verb** agrees with the **subject** in both parts of the sentence.

Hint #2:

If a sentence doesn't sound right to you, it may be because it has a mistake in it!

Answer: Choice **C** is correct.

Because the first part of the sentence has a **compound subject**, meaning there's more than one person or thing in the subject, the verb must be in the correct form. *Are going* is correct, because *are* agrees with the compound subject, *Esmay, Matthew, and Nikhil*. The correct choice is *to see Matthew's brother play,* so choice **C** is correct.

14. What is the **best** way to write the **underlined** part of the sentence?

Harry <u>will ride</u> his bicycle to the park with Bert yesterday.

Ⓐ has ridden

Ⓑ is riding

Ⓒ rode

Ⓓ rides

Hint #1:

The verb should agree with the subject, and be in the correct **tense**, past, present or future.

Hint #2:

Look for clues in the sentence that show when the action in the sentence happened or will happen.

Answer: Choice **C** is correct.

The sentence should read: **Harry <u>rode</u> his bicycle to the park with Bert yesterday**. Because the sentence contains the word *yesterday*, you know that it should be written in the past tense.

15. Choose the best way to write the **underlined** part of the sentence.

When I get to the city next week, I <u>have gone</u> straight to my friend's house.

(A) will go

(B) go

(C) went

(D) are going

Hint #1:

Read the first part of the sentence carefully to get clues about the **verb tense**.

Hint #2:

Remember, it sometimes helps to try out each answer choice in the sentence and see which one fits best.

Answer: Choice **A** is correct.

The sentence should read: **When I get to the city next week, I will go straight to my friend's house**. Because the speaker is referring to a specific time in the future, the future tense of the verb **will go** is best.

16. What is the **subject** of the following sentence?

Earlier in the week, the boys decided to get all of their homework done so that they could go to the game.

(A) week

(B) boys

(C) decided

(D) homework

Hint #1:

Think about **who** or **what** is performing the action in the sentence.

Hint #2:

Keep in mind that the subject of a sentence is either the noun that is performing the action or the noun that the sentence is about.

Answer: Choice **B** is correct.

In this sentence, *boys* is the subject. The **boys** decided to get their homework done, so the boys are performing the action.

17. Which word from the sentence below is an **adjective**?

I had a delicious lunch at Patty's famous restaurant with my great friends Sara and Wendy, and then Sara had to leave quickly to get to her piano lesson.

(A) lunch

(B) famous

(C) lesson

(D) quickly

Hint #1:

Think about what kind of word an adjective describes.

Hint #2:

An **adjective** is a word that modifies, or describes, a **noun**.

Answer: Choice **B** is correct.

The word *famous* is an **adjective**. In the sentence, *famous* modifies the noun *restaurant*, because it tells what kind of restaurant it is. An adjective is a word that modifies, or describes, a noun. Some of the questions that an adjective answers are: **Which one**? **What kind**? **How many**? The only word in the answer choices that describes a noun is the word *famous*.

18. Which word from the sentence below is an **adverb**?

Slowly and carefully, Wanda removed the blue cover from the top of the wet pail.

(A) slowly

(B) Wanda

(C) moved

(D) blue

Hint #1:

Think about what kinds of words adverbs modify.

Hint #2:

An **adverb** is a word that modifies a **verb**, an **adjective**, or another **adverb**.

Answer: Choice **A** is correct.

The word *slowly* is an **adverb**. An **adverb** is a word that modifies a **verb**, an **adjective**, or another **adverb**. In this sentence, *slowly* tells how Wanda removed the blue cover, so **slowly** is an **adverb** modifying the verb *removed*. Some of the questions that an adverb answers are: **How**? **When**? **Why**? **Under what conditions**? and **To what extent**?

19. Choose the correct form of the verb *"to be"* for the blank in the following sentence.

Every time Stephen looks at the clouds, he imagines he _____ flying a huge jet plane.

(A) are

(B) be

(C) is

(D) was

Hint #1:

Use the first part of the sentence to find clues about the proper tense of the verb.

Hint #2:

Remember, it sometimes helps to try out each answer choice in the sentence and see which one fits best.

Answer: Choice **C** is correct.

The sentence should read: **Every time Stephen looks at the clouds, he imagines he is flying a huge jet plane**. The verb should be in **present tense**, because it is referring to an action that happens **frequently** and **continuously**. It should also be in **singular form** to go with the word *he*. Choice **C**, is the form of *to be* that is both in **present tense** and **singular form.**

Challenge Activity

You're doing a great job so far!
Are you ready for a Challenge Activity?
Good luck!

a) Underline the **direct objects** in the following sentences.

1. Paul and Veronica filled the pool with water.

2. I dumped my homework on the table.

3. Sara put her glasses down.

b) Underline the **indirect objects** in the following sentences.

1. Marcia loaned me her bike.

2. Jeffrey bought Meg a deck of cards.

3. Mrs. Holtz taught everyone how to spell "cheese."

c) What is the **best** way to write the **underlined** part of the sentence?

Beth <u>finish</u> all of her chores before going to the park yesterday afternoon.

Ⓐ will finish

Ⓑ finished

Ⓒ finishes

Ⓓ finishing

Hint #1:

Direct objects and **indirect objects** help to make sentences more detailed and complete.

Hint #2:

Direct objects come after the verb and answer the question "**What**?" The **indirect object** is closely related to the direct object and answers the questions "**To what**?" or "**To whom**?"

Answers to Challenge Activity:

a) Did you find all of the direct objects?

1. Paul and Veronica filled the <u>pool</u> with water.

2. I dumped my <u>homework</u> on the table.

3. Sara put her <u>glasses</u> down.

When finding the **direct object**, be sure to find the verb, and then ask yourself "**what**?" For example, in **sentence 1**, ask, "**What did they fill**?" In **sentence 2**, ask, "**What did I dump**?" In **sentence 3**, ask, "**What did she put**?"

b) Did you find all of the indirect objects?

1. Marcia loaned <u>me</u> her bike.

2. Jeffrey bought <u>Meg</u> a deck of cards.

3. Mrs. Holtz taught <u>everyone</u> how to spell "cheese."

An **indirect object** precedes the direct object and tells **to whom** or **for whom** the action of the verb is done and who is receiving the direct object. There must be a direct object to have an indirect object. Indirect objects are usually found with verbs of giving or communicating like **give**, **bring**, **tell**, **show**, **take**, or **offer**.

c) Choice **B** is correct.

The correct way to write the sentence is: **Beth <u>finished</u> all of her chores before going to the park yesterday afternoon**.

The sentence should be written in the **past tense**, including the verb. The past tense of the word **finish** is **finished**.

Let's take a quick test and see how much you've learned during this climb up SCORE! Mountain.

Good luck!

1. Which of the following underlined words is an adjective?

   The <u>brown</u> collie and <u>loudly</u> barking <u>terrier</u> <u>chased</u> the cat into the shady <u>trees</u>.

   (A) brown

   (B) loudly

   (C) terrier

   (D) chased

2. Which of the choices in the sentences below has a capitalization error?

   <u>Matt</u> had to go to the <u>Grocery</u> <u>Store</u> for his <u>mom</u>. He went to
     Ⓐ   Ⓑ   Ⓒ

   Amos's Gourmet <u>Goods</u> down the <u>block</u>.
   Ⓓ   Ⓔ

3. Which of the following is the correct way to punctuate the underlined part of the sentence below?

   I had a great <u>time last night I went</u> to a party with my friend Sue.

   (A) time last night, I went

   (B) time, last night; I went

   (C) time last night; I went,

   (D) time last night; I went

4. Which of the following best completes the sentence?

Angela and her friend _____ the puppy to the park the other day.

(A) takes

(B) is taking

(C) are taking

(D) took

5. Which part of the following sentence contains an error in punctuation?

"We decided to go to the football <u>game today</u> instead of next <u>week"</u>
(A)   (B)   (C)

<u>said</u> <u>Joey happily.</u>
(D)   (E)

Answers to test questions:

1. Choice **A** is correct.
An **adjective** is a word that describes a **noun**. **Brown** is the only one of the words that describes a **noun**, **collie**.

2. Choice **B** is correct.
Only nouns that are **proper nouns**—they name a specific person, place, or thing—should be capitalized. The phrase **grocery store** is not naming a specific store, so it should **not** be capitalized.

3. Choice **D** is correct.
The two phrases "**I had a great time last night**" and "**I went to a party with my friend Sue**" are **independent clauses,** which means they are complete sentences on their own, so they should be separated with a **semicolon**. The phrases don't need any commas added. The sentence should be written as follows: **I had a great time last night; I went to a party with my friend Sue**.

4. Choice **D** is correct.
The **verb** should agree with the **compound subject**—*Angela and her friend*—and should also be in **past tense** because of the phrase **the other day**. Only choice **D** is in past tense and agrees with the subject. The sentence should read: **Angela and her friend <u>took</u> the puppy to the park the other day**.

5. Choice **C** is correct.
Put a **comma** after what someone says, and before the quotation marks. In part **C** of the sentence, the comma should be placed after the word **week**, before the quotation marks, as follows: "**We decided to go to the football game today instead of next week<u>,</u>" said Joey happily**.

Celebrate!

Let's take a fun break before we go to the next base camp. You've earned it!

Sometimes, studying hard can make you hungry.

How about a delicious snack for a fun study break?

Let's make some gelatin!

You will need:

• A box of gelatin—there are lots of great flavors, pick your favorite!

• Boiling water—ask a parent or guardian for permission or help with using the stove or microwave oven to boil water

• Some cups to pour your gelatin into

• Anything you'd like to add to your gelatin, such as fruit, marshmallows, whipped cream, and sprinkles

Congratulations!
You're halfway to the top of *SCORE!* Mountain.

Directions:

- Gelatin is really easy to make; all you need is a box of gelatin and boiling water.
- Maybe you have a box of gelatin in your house already. If not, ask a parent or guardian to get you some.
- Ask a parent or guardian for permission or help with using the stove or microwave oven to boil water.
- Follow the directions on the box carefully, and have fun making your delicious snack!
- Get creative and add fruit, marshmallows, whipped cream, and sprinkles, or whatever you like to make your snack even better!
- Put your gelatin in fun cups!
- Share your delicious snack with friends and family!

Good luck and have fun!
You deserve it for working so hard!

Base Camp

4

Reading Nonfiction

Wow! You're getting close to the top of *SCORE!* Mountain. Are you ready for another fun climb? Let's get started! Good luck!

SCORE! MOUNTAIN TOP

BASE CAMP 5

BASE CAMP 4

BASE CAMP 3

BASE CAMP 2

BASE CAMP 1

1. Which of the following statements is an **opinion**?

Ⓐ Even though tigers are considered dangerous, many people keep them as pets.

Ⓑ A tiger is a beautiful animal.

Ⓒ Tigers often hunt on their own instead of in packs.

Ⓓ Tigers are the biggest cats in the world.

Hint #1:

Opinions are personal beliefs, ideas, or thoughts. Even though we may disagree with an opinion, we cannot **prove** it to be true or false.

Hint #2:

Look for the statement that **cannot** be proven to be true.

Answer: Choice **B** is correct.

The only statement that cannot be proven using science or observation is: **A tiger is a beautiful animal**. Some may agree with this statement and some may disagree, but it is an **opinion**, not a fact.

2. Which of the following statements is a **fact**?

    (A) Baseball is the most incredible spectator sport.

    (B) Baseball fans are, without a doubt, the most enthusiastic sports fans of all.

    (C) The best baseball player of all time was Babe Ruth.

    (D) Baseball is a game that you can watch on television.

Hint #1:

Facts can be proven to be true.

Hint #2:

Facts can be proven to be true by **doing research** or **making observations**.

Answer: Choice **D** is correct.

Only choice **D** cannot be disagreed with. Because opinion statements represent an opinion or belief, someone can agree with them or disagree with them. It is a fact that **baseball is a game that you can watch on television.**

3. Which of the following types of reading materials is **not** a type of **nonfiction**?

(A) a newspaper article

(B) a science textbook

(C) a fairy tale

(D) a cookbook

Hint #1:

In **nonfiction** material, the author **retells true events** or **gives factual information**. Think about which of the reading materials is not retelling **true events**.

Hint #2:

Which of the answer choices probably doesn't contain **factual information**?

Answer: Choice **C** is correct.

A **fairy tale** does not retell true events, so it is a type of **fiction**, not nonfiction. **Nonfiction** reading can be found in many places, such as on certain websites on the Internet, in different types of books, and in magazines and newspapers.

Read the following passage carefully, then answer questions 4–7.

The second president of the United States of America was John Adams. His life began in Braintree, Massachusetts, on October 30th, 1735. When he was a young man, Adams went to Harvard University to study law. After he graduated, he became concerned with the cause of the American patriots, and he went on to become a leader in the colonies' move for independence. He was also a diplomat; during the Revolutionary War, he helped to negotiate peace treaties in France and Holland. He returned to the United States because he was elected to be vice president under George Washington. Adams also served two terms as president, but this time was the low point of his political career. He once said to his wife Abigail Adams that he did not enjoy being president. After his presidency was over, he retired to his farm. He died on July 4, 1826, in the same town where he was born.

4. Which of the following would be the **best title** for the passage?

Ⓐ The early career of John Adams

Ⓑ John Adams, Foreign Diplomat

Ⓒ The relationship between John Adams and his wife, Abigail

Ⓓ John Adams' Political Career

Hint #1:

Look for the answer choice that gives the **main idea** of the passage in a clear and straightforward manner.

Hint #2:

Eliminate choices that are about only one detail from the passage, and look for a title that best explains the passage as a whole.

Answer: Choice **D** is correct.

John Adams' Political Career would be the best title for the passage. The passage as a whole is a brief summary of the political career of John Adams, and choice **D** says exactly that.

5. Why did John Adams return to the United States after serving as a diplomat?

    (A) He was unhappy with his job overseas.

    (B) He returned to fight in the Revolutionary War.

    (C) He was elected vice president.

    (D) He wanted to return to his home in Braintree, Massachusetts.

Hint #1:

This question is asking about a **specific detail** from the passage.

Hint #2:

If you're not sure of the answer, it's a good strategy to go back and reread the part of the passage that the question refers to.

Answer: Choice **C** is correct.

First, find the part of the passage that explains why Adams returned to the United States after serving as a diplomat. Here is the sentence that will help you to find the information: "*He returned to the United States because he was elected to be vice president under George Washington.*" Choice **C** is the correct answer.

6. In what city did John Adams die?

Ⓐ Braintree, Massachusetts

Ⓑ Boston, Massachusetts

Ⓒ Washington, D.C.

Ⓓ Paris, France

Hint #1:

First, find the place in the passage that tells where John Adams died.

Hint #2:

Then, check the location carefully with details from the beginning of the passage.

Answer: Choice **A** is correct.

John Adams died in **Braintree, Massachusetts**. In the last line, the passage says that John Adams died *in the same town where he was born*. Be sure to check the passage carefully to review where he was born; don't just rely on memory. The second line of the passage says that Adams' life began in **Braintree, Massachusetts**, meaning he was born there.

7. Based on the passage, which of the following is **most likely true** about the career of John Adams?

(A) Adams is considered to be the most successful president.

(B) Adams did not agree with George Washington on many political issues.

(C) Adams enjoyed being a foreign diplomat more than being the president.

(D) Adams believed that the colonies should not declare independence from Britain.

Hint #1:

Even though the correct answer may not be stated directly in the passage, it should be supported by **details** from the passage.

Hint #2:

Eliminate any answer choices that cannot be supported by evidence in the passage.

Answer: Choice **C** is correct.

Choice **C**, that **Adams enjoyed being a diplomat more than he enjoyed being president**, is supported in the text, because it says that being president was *the low point of his political career*, and that **he told his wife** *that he did not enjoy being president*. If being president was the low point of his career, **it makes sense** that Adams enjoyed being a foreign diplomat **more** than he enjoyed being president. We do not have any evidence that supports the other answer choices.

© Kaplan Publishing, Inc.

Read the passage carefully, then answer questions 8–11.

Jupiter is the fifth planet from the sun. In the early 1600s, the scientist Galileo was the first to observe the four moons orbiting Jupiter, which led him to agree with the unpopular theory that the planets orbit the sun. The four moons of Jupiter are named Io, Europa, Ganymede, and Calisto. Jupiter is what is known as a gas giant, because it does not have a solid surface. Jupiter is made up of 90 percent hydrogen and 10 percent oxygen, with very small amounts of other substances, such as rock, methane, and water. Jupiter is easily recognizable in pictures because of its Giant Red Spot, or GRS. The GRS was first observed in the late 1600s. Scientists believe that it is an area of high pressure, with higher and colder clouds than the rest of the planet. They are not certain why the clouds have remained this way for so long. One of the most amazing characteristics of Jupiter is its size. Jupiter is so large that its mass is twice that of all of the other planets combined.

8. Which of the following **best** describes the **main idea** of the passage?

Ⓐ Galileo's discovery of Jupiter's moons

Ⓑ the planet Jupiter

Ⓒ Jupiter's Giant Red Spot

Ⓓ the planets in the solar system

Hint #1:

Remember, **main idea** questions are asking about the passage as a whole.

Hint #2:

It may help to reread the passage in order to figure out which answer choice best captures what it is about.

Answer: Choice **B** is correct.

The passage gives facts about different aspects of the planet **Jupiter**, so the best choice for the main idea of the passage is simply, *the planet Jupiter*.

9. Which of the following **best describes** why the author probably wrote this passage?

(A) To argue that Galileo's theories about the solar system were correct

(B) To introduce new evidence about Jupiter's atmosphere

(C) To point out how little scientists understand about Jupiter

(D) To give the reader general information about Jupiter

Hint #1:

Think about why the author might have written this passage, and what he or she wanted the reader to understand.

Hint #2:

Eliminate any answer choices that aren't supported by details in the passage.

Answer: Choice **D** is correct.

In this passage, the writer has a very informative style, as if it came from a textbook. The author does not add her own opinions in the article; she mostly presents facts. The best choice for the author's purpose, therefore, is choice **D**, *to give the reader general information about Jupiter*.

10. Which of the following is **not** the name of one of Jupiter's moons?

(A) Galileo

(B) Europa

(C) Ganymede

(D) Io

Hint #1:

Find and reread the section of the passage that tells about Jupiter's moons.

Hint #2:

Eliminate any answer choices that aren't supported by details in the passage.

Answer: Choice **A** is correct.

Galileo is **not** the name of one of Jupiter's moons. Lines 3–4 of the passage discuss the moons of Jupiter. *Galileo* is the scientist who observed them, **not** one of the moons. Be sure to go back and reread the passage; the question becomes much easier if you use the passage to help you!

11. According to the passage, which of the following is **not** likely true about the GRS?

Ⓐ Scientists did not know it existed before the late 1600s.

Ⓑ It has lower temperatures than the rest of the planet.

Ⓒ It is made up of clouds.

Ⓓ The clouds remain this way because cold air is dense and stays in the same area.

Hint #1:
First, carefully reread the section of the passage about the GRS.

Hint #2:
Check each answer choice with the information given in the passage.

Answer: Choice **D** is correct.

Looking at choice **D**, the passage says that scientists **don't know** why the clouds remain in the same area, so we **don't know** if it's because of the dense cold air. Choice **D** is most likely not true.

Read the following recipe carefully and then answer questions 12–15.

Grandma's World-Famous Peanut Butter Chip Cookies

3 cups flour

$\frac{1}{2}$ teaspoon baking soda

$\frac{1}{4}$ teaspoon salt

1 stick butter, softened

2 eggs

$\frac{3}{4}$ cup brown sugar

$\frac{3}{4}$ cup white sugar

$\frac{1}{4}$ teaspoon cinnamon

16 ounces peanut butter chips

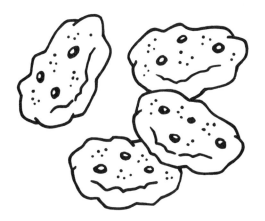

Preheat the oven to 375°. In a medium mixing bowl, stir together the flour, baking soda, and salt. Set aside. In a large mixing bowl, combine the butter, brown sugar, white sugar, and cinnamon. Beat on a medium-high setting until well mixed. Beat in the eggs. Slowly stir the flour mixture into the butter mixture. Once the entire flour mixture has been added, mix for 5 minutes. Stir in the peanut butter chips. Spoon tablespoon-sized pieces of cookie batter onto a greased cookie sheet. Bake for 10–15 minutes. Baking time may vary, depending on oven heat. Let cookies cool for 10 minutes before eating.

12. Based on the passage, which choice gives the **best** explanation for why someone would bake the cookies for **10 minutes** instead of **15 minutes**?

- (A) He or she didn't follow the directions carefully.
- (B) He or she has a smaller oven.
- (C) He or she is making fewer cookies.
- (D) He or she has a hotter oven.

Hint #1:

Find and read the part of the passage that tells about baking the cookies.

Hint #2:

Remember to eliminate answer choices that do not seem to fit or make sense.

Answer: Choice **D** is correct.

The answer to this question can be found toward the end of the directions. The baking times *vary, depending on oven heat*, meaning that depending on how hot the oven is, the cookies will have to be baked for a **longer** or **shorter** period of time, so choice **D** is correct.

13. According to the directions, what should you do **right after** you preheat the oven?

(A) Stir together the flour, baking soda, and salt.

(B) Wash a medium mixing bowl.

(C) Stir in the peanut butter chips.

(D) Grease the cookie sheet.

Hint #1:

Use the passage to help you! Go back to the passage and review what you should do right after you preheat the oven.

Hint #2:

Make sure you follow the correct order of the recipe's directions.

Answer: Choice **A** is correct.

Right after you preheat the oven, you should **stir together the flour, baking soda, and salt**. According to the passage, choice **A** is the next step. For questions such as this, where the answer can be found directly in the passage, it's important to go back and check the passage.

14. Which of the following is the **most likely** reason for someone to read this passage?

Ⓐ to learn about Grandma's life

Ⓑ to learn to carefully follow directions

Ⓒ to find out how to make peanut butter chip cookies

Ⓓ to think about his or her favorite foods

Hint #1:

Think about why you might find this passage useful in your own life.

Hint #2:

Eliminate the answer choices that don't seem to be likely reasons for reading a cookie recipe.

Answer: Choice **C** is correct.

The most likely reason for someone to read this passage is **to find out how to make peanut butter chip cookies**.

Reading is a powerful tool that we use all the time, and one important kind of nonfiction reading is reading to understand how to make or do something. Being able to read and follow a set of instructions is a very valuable skill!

© Kaplan Publishing, Inc.

15. This passage would **most likely** be found

    Ⓐ in an encyclopedia.

    Ⓑ in an atlas.

    Ⓒ on a recipe website.

    Ⓓ in a book of fiction.

Hint #1:

Think about where this passage would most likely be found, and then check each choice one at a time, looking for a choice that matches your prediction.

Hint #2:

What type of information would you find in each of the answer choices?

Answer: Choice **C** is correct.

This passage, a cookie recipe, would most likely be found **on a recipe website**. Upon first reading this question, you may have thought to yourself that the most likely place to find this passage is in a **cookbook**. That response makes sense, and **predicting an answer** before you get to the choices is often a very useful strategy. After reviewing the answer choices, choice **C**, *on a recipe website*, is most similar to a cookbook and is the right answer.

Read the following passage, then answer questions 16–19.

The Unusual Kiwi

When many people hear the word *kiwi*, they think of a green fruit with black seeds and a fuzzy skin. However, kiwi also has a different meaning. "Kiwi" is also a kind of bird. The kiwi bird is a brown bird from New Zealand. The kiwi is a very special bird because it is one of the few birds in the world that is flightless, meaning it cannot fly.

However, that's not the only reason that the kiwi is unique. Even though the kiwi's beak looks very long, scientists actually consider it to have a very short beak. This is because a kiwi's nostrils are at the *end* of its beak. The kiwi's nostrils are at the end of its beak to help it to poke around in the underbrush, looking for food.

The kiwi is also an unusual bird because its eggs are very large. Kiwis are about the same size as chickens, but kiwi eggs are about the same size as ostrich eggs. Incredible, right?

Another interesting fact about kiwis is that they are nocturnal, so they have an unusual sleep schedule. They only come out at night to search for food so that they won't be as endangered by predators. They sleep during the day in hidden burrows.

Speaking of endangered, the kiwi bird is an endangered species, meaning kiwis are in danger of extinction. They are threatened by predators, which are mostly animals that are not native to New Zealand but were brought over by people. The kiwi is also threatened by loss of its habitat. People are developing so much land that the kiwi is losing places where it can live. To find out what you can do to help kiwis, do some research online. There are many great websites that tell about how to protect this amazing bird.

16. What is the meaning of the word *nocturnal*?

(A) having a diet of bugs and fruit

(B) having nostrils on the end of the beak

(C) flightless

(D) coming out at night

Hint #1:

If you're not sure of what the word means, go back and reread the paragraph containing the word *nocturnal*.

Hint #2:

What does this paragraph tell us about the kiwi?

Answer: Choice **D** is correct.

Nocturnal means **coming out at night**. Even though the paragraph does have a sentence about the kiwi's diet, the paragraph is mainly about why the kiwi searches for food at night.

17. This passage is mainly about

    Ⓐ native birds of New Zealand.

    Ⓑ what makes the kiwi unique.

    Ⓒ the importance of protecting endangered species.

    Ⓓ differences between the kiwi bird and the kiwi fruit.

Hint #1:

You can often use the **title** of a nonfiction passage to help you with a main idea question like this one.

Hint #2:

Remember that you can always reread the passage to refresh your memory about what the passage is mainly about.

Answer: Choice **B** is correct.

This passage is mainly about **what makes the kiwi unique**.

Titles of nonfiction selections can often help to provide a sense of the main idea of the passage, or what the passage is primarily about. The title, **The Unusual Kiwi**, tells us that the passage will explain what makes the kiwi **unusual**, or *unique*.

18. Which of the following is **not** a characteristic of a kiwi bird?

(A) Having a diet of bugs and fruit

(B) Having a brown color

(C) Being flightless

(D) Being able to swim

Hint #1:

Because the question doesn't give you any clues about where to look in the passage to find the answer, check each choice carefully!

Hint #2:

Eliminate choices that are mentioned in the passage as characteristics.

Answer: Choice **D** is correct.

Being able to swim is **not** a characteristic of a kiwi bird. Be sure that you think about what is **not** mentioned as a characteristic; otherwise, all the other answer choices might be tempting!

19. The author would **probably agree** with which of the
following statements?

Ⓐ The kiwi bird is a pest to farmers.

Ⓑ Kiwis are not as grand a bird as the mighty ostrich.

Ⓒ The kiwi is an interesting bird and should be protected.

Ⓓ The penguin is another unusual flightless bird.

Hint #1:

Think about the author's
tone and why she might have
written the passage.

Hint #2:

Is there information in the
passage that would lead you
to think that the author would
probably agree with one of the
answer choices?

Answer: Choice **C** is correct.

The author would probably agree that *the kiwi is an interesting bird and
should be protected*. The final part of the passage provides the most clues
about this question. The author even provides information about how to
help protect the kiwi. The passage is written in a tone of respect for the kiwi
and of fascination with its interesting qualities.

You're doing a great job so far!
Are you ready for a Challenge Activity?
Good luck!

This passage is a little longer and more complex than some of the other passages in this workbook. Do your best to read carefully, and stop to reread the passage or sentences if you need to! Answer the questions that follow.

A Great Man

Dr. Martin Luther King, Jr., was born on January 15, 1929 in Atlanta, Georgia. Although the name Michael Luther was listed on his birth certificate, King went by the name Martin Luther. King followed in his father's and his grandfather's footsteps by graduating from Morehouse College with a Bachelor of Arts degree in 1948. Next, he went on to study at Crozer Theological Seminary, where he was elected president of his senior class. King went on to attend Boston University, where he received a PhD in Theology and met his wife, Coretta Scott.

Coretta Scott and King were married on June 18, 1953. King's father performed the wedding ceremony at Coretta's parents' house in Alabama. They had four children: two boys (Martin Luther III and Dexter) and two girls (Yolanda and Bernice).

Dr. Martin Luther King, Jr. is perhaps best known for his work for civil rights and equal rights for all citizens. On December 1, 1955, history was made when Rosa Parks, a black woman, refused to give up her seat on a bus to a white man. King got involved by leading the Montgomery Bus Boycott, which lasted for 382 days. King encouraged people to boycott, or to stop riding, the buses. His goal was for the bus companies to lose money, and be forced to treat people more fairly. During this time, King's house was bombed, and he was arrested. The

end result of the boycott, however, was more positive for King. The United States Supreme Court said that it was illegal to force people to sit in a certain section of the bus because of their race, meaning that blacks no longer had to give up their seats for whites.

After the bus boycott, King helped to create the Southern Christian Leadership Conference, or SCLC. The purpose of this group was to unite black churches to protest peacefully the unfair treatment of blacks and to work for civil rights for all citizens. From 1957 to 1968, King led this organization and traveled throughout the country, speaking out against injustice. One of King's most famous speeches is his "I Have a Dream" speech, which he gave in Washington, DC. He also wrote books and many articles expressing his views.

When he was only thirty-five, King was awarded the Nobel Peace Prize for his work for civil rights. He gave the prize money of over $50,000 to the civil rights movement. He was named *Time Magazine*'s Man of the Year in 1963. Then, on April 4, 1968, at the age of thirty-nine, King was killed in Memphis, Tennessee. He was a truly great leader whose work will always be remembered.

Write your answers to the following questions on the lines below.

    a) What did Dr. King do that his father and grandfather also did?

_____

_____

_____

_____

    b) According to the passage, what was the **positive outcome** of the Montgomery Bus Boycott?

_____

_____

_____

_____

    c) Based on the information in the passage, why might King have been named *Time Magazine*'s Man of the Year in 1963?

_____

_____

_____

_____

Answers to Challenge Activity:

Everyone's answers to these questions will look different. See if you have the same basic ideas as the answers below. If so, then your answers are likely correct too!

a) **Like his father and grandfather, Martin Luther King, Jr. graduated with a degree from Morehouse College.** To find the answer, find the part of the passage that talks about King's father and grandfather. In paragraph 1, the passage says that King *followed in his father and grandfather's footsteps* by graduating from Morehouse College.

b) **The positive outcome for King was that the United States Supreme Court decided to outlaw racial segregation on buses and all public transportation.** You can find this answer at the end of paragraph three.

c) **King might have been named *Time Magazine*'s Man of the Year in 1963 for his work for civil rights, or possibly for donating his Nobel Prize money to the civil rights movement.**

Let's take a quick test and see how much you've learned during this climb up SCORE! Mountain.

Good luck!

Read the following passage, then answer the questions.

Lake Michigan is one of the five Great Lakes located in North America. Lake Michigan is the only one of the five lakes that is located entirely within the borders of the United States; the other Great Lakes share a border with Canada. Lake Michigan is bordered by four states: Michigan, Illinois, Indiana, and Wisconsin, and is the largest freshwater lake in the United States and the fifth largest in the world. The largest city located on the border of Lake Michigan is Chicago, with a population of nearly three million. Chicago is a city famous for its elevated trains and delicious pizza.

Lake Michigan is famous for one of its most beautiful features, its sand dunes. These sand dunes are large hills of sand, which are caused by strong winds from the west. The sand dunes contribute to the overall beauty of Lake Michigan's beaches, especially in Indiana and Michigan. The sand dunes are home to a variety of plant and animal life, and are a major part of the ecosystem in these areas. Lake Michigan is truly different from the other Great Lakes, and its surrounding beaches are arguably the most beautiful freshwater beaches in the world.

Because of its beauty and location, Lake Michigan is a popular tourist destination. People from all around the world visit its beaches to water-ski, hike on the sand dunes, or simply relax on the beach. There are many state and national parks along the lakeshore that tourists can visit. Tourists can also sign up for guided boat tours of the lake, or walking tours of the sand dunes. Most of the beaches are open year-round and are fun to visit in the winter as well as the summer.

1. According to the passage, which of the following facts makes Lake Michigan different from the other Great Lakes?

    (A) It has no sand dunes.

    (B) It borders one of the largest cities in the United States.

    (C) It is located entirely within the borders of the United States.

    (D) It has a longer name.

2. Which of the following is the passage about?

    (A) The Great Lakes

    (B) Lake Michigan's Sand Dunes

    (C) Fresh Water Lakes

    (D) Lake Michigan

3. Which of the following is an opinion from the passage?

    (A) Lake Michigan is bordered by four states: Michigan, Illinois, Indiana, and Wisconsin, and is the largest freshwater lake in the United States and the fifth largest in the world.

    (B) The largest city located on the border of Lake Michigan is Chicago, with a population of nearly three million.

    (C) These sand dunes are large hills of sand, which are caused by strong winds from the west.

    (D) The sand dunes contribute to the overall beauty of Lake Michigan's beaches, especially in Indiana and Michigan.

4. Which of the following sentences does not belong in paragraph 1?

Ⓐ Lake Michigan is one of the five Great Lakes located in North America.

Ⓑ Lake Michigan is the only one of the five lakes that is located entirely within the borders of the United States; the other Great Lakes share a border with Canada.

Ⓒ Lake Michigan is bordered by four states: Michigan, Illinois, Indiana, and Wisconsin, and is the largest freshwater lake in the United States and the fifth largest in the world.

Ⓓ Chicago is a city famous for its elevated trains and delicious pizza.

5. According to the passage, which is a reason that a tourist would visit Lake Michigan?

Ⓐ to go fishing

Ⓑ to eat delicious pizza

Ⓒ to hike on the sand dunes

Ⓓ to go snorkeling

Answers to test questions:

1. Choice **C** is correct.

You can find the answer to this question in the passage's second sentence: "***Lake Michigan is the only one of the five lakes that is located entirely within the borders of the United States; the other Great Lakes share a border with Canada.***"

2. Choice **D** is correct.

The passage is about ***Lake Michigan***. Choices **A** and **C** are too general; the passage isn't about all of the Great Lakes or all freshwater lakes, it's about one lake in particular, Lake Michigan. Choice **B** is **too specific**. Choice **D** is just right.

3. Choice **D** is correct.

You couldn't really prove that choice **D** is true, because we can't really prove that something is ***beautiful***. It's an **opinion**. In fact, some people might disagree because they don't think the sand dunes are beautiful!

4. Choice **D** is correct.

Paragraph 1 gives general facts about Lake Michigan. Choice **D** is really about Chicago, not Lake Michigan, so it doesn't belong in the paragraph.

5. Choice **C** is correct.

The best answer is choice **C** because it is mentioned right in sentence 2 of paragraph 3. A reason that a tourist would visit Lake Michigan is to ***hike on the sand dunes***.

Celebrate!

Let's take a fun break before we go to the next base camp. You've earned it!

Do you have a favorite game?

Maybe it's a board game or a card game, or maybe it's a video game?

Congratulations! You're getting closer to the top of *SCORE!* Mountain.

Playing a game is a fun break from studying, and a lot of fun, as long as you make sure that you still leave time to do all of your schoolwork and chores!

Take some time out from studying and play your favorite game as a reward for doing so well in this work session!

Good luck and have fun!

You deserve it for working so hard!

Base Camp

5

Reading Fiction

You are really getting close to the top of *SCORE!* Mountain. Great work! Let's keep going! Good luck!

SCORE! MOUNTAIN TOP

BASE CAMP 5

BASE CAMP 4

BASE CAMP 3

BASE CAMP 2

BASE CAMP 1

1. Which of the following is an example of **fiction writing**?

(A) a dictionary

(B) a restaurant menu

(C) a fairy tale

(D) a phone book

Hint #1:

Fiction is a type of writing that is based on the author's ideas or imagination.

Hint #2:

Fiction is not necessarily based on real facts.

Answer: Choice **C** is correct.

A **fairy tale** is an example of **fiction writing**.

Fairy tales often contain some kind of magic, and often involve one character changing from something to something else completely different, like when a princess kisses a frog and it turns into a prince!

Read the following passage, then answer question 2.

A mystery story usually has the following types of characters: a **detective** (sometimes known as a **sleuth**), a **victim**, a **villain**, and sometimes an **assistant for the detective**. The characters should be **believable**, meaning they don't do anything that's really **wacky** or **unexpected**, and they should **act in predictable ways**.

2. Read the following **character names and descriptions**. Which of the following characters does **not** sound like a typical mystery character?

- (A) Inspector Laroche, experienced super sleuth
- (B) Janet Darkcloak, famous jewel thief
- (C) Mrs. Thurmond, rich heiress whose diamond necklace was stolen
- (D) Jillian Moore, news reporter

Hint #1:

What **characters** are usually in a mystery story?

Hint #2:

Have you ever read a mystery story? What kinds of characters did it have in it?

Answer: Choice **D** is correct.

Jillian Moore, news reporter, does **not** sound like a typical mystery character. According to the information in the passage, the other answer choices are characters that you would typically find in a mystery story.

Read the short passage below, then answer question 3.

A mystery story has a problem that the detective is trying to solve. Many mysteries begin with a crime, and the detective in the story tries to figure out who did it. A mystery should give the reader clues that he or she can use to try to solve the puzzle.

3. Based on what you just read in the passage, which would not be a very good **title** for a mystery story?

Ⓐ The Case of the Missing Necklace

Ⓑ The Secret of the Dark Cave

Ⓒ The Cute Dog and the Speedy Cat

Ⓓ The Perfect Crime

Hint #1:

Think about what a mystery story is about.

Hint #2:

Imagine finding a book with each of the titles in the answer choices. Which title **least** sounds as if it will be about solving a problem?

Answer: Choice **C** is correct.

The Cute Dog and the Speedy Cat doesn't sound like a good title for a mystery story. Remember, mystery stories usually have a problem, crime, or puzzle that a detective is trying to solve. Does *The Cute Dog and the Speedy Cat* sound as if it would be about that?

Read the following short story carefully and then answer questions 4–7.

Colin had a pit in his stomach. He was riding the school bus on his way to the first day of school, and this year he would be attending The Academy of the Arts and Sciences, a school his parents were thrilled about. It was his fourth school in three years, and he hoped he could stay long enough to get past the part where the kids teased him every day. The teasing always started when attendance was called. Colin had a last name that everyone thought was funny. It was bad enough being the new kid, but being the new kid *and* having a last name like his was unbearable. He had a routine; he would simply ignore the teasing and act like it didn't bother him, and then suggest a game of kickball at recess where he could *showcase* his brilliant skills. After that, the kids usually left him alone.

Colin's thoughts were interrupted by a loud, very close voice coming from behind him. "Hey!" called the voice. "Hey, who are you?"

Colin sighed and turned around. "Name's Colin. Who are you?"

"I'm Becky, and I know everyone that comes on this bus. In fact, I pretty much control this bus. I'm not sure you belong on here. But, there might be one way you can get to stay. If you can beat me in a one-on-one kickball match, you are allowed on this bus for the rest of the year. You have one chance, and one chance only, and it's today at lunch. If you lose, well, let's just say I hope your parents like to drive." Becky Yearling was the ruler of the bus; in fact, she was the ruler of the school. Everyone was afraid of her, and rightly so. She was at least a head taller than anyone else was and had the attitude to go with her height. She was also the school's kickball star.

Luckily, Colin knew that he was in the clear. A kickball contest was one contest he knew he could win. He gave Becky a sly half-smile. "You're on."

© Kaplan Publishing, Inc.

Becky looked surprised, but she returned Colin's grin and put her hand out for a shake. "You've got guts, kid, I'll give you that." And with that, she stomped off to the back of the bus to join her devoted crew.

Colin smiled to himself. The day wasn't starting out half bad after all.

4. What does the word *showcase* mean in the story?

(A) stump

(B) display

(C) prevent

(D) explain

Hint #1:

Go back to the story and find the word ***showcase***.

Hint #2:

Think about why the kids would decide to leave Colin alone after the kickball game. Be sure to read the sentence from the story again, inserting the choices to see which one makes the most sense.

Answer: Choice **B** is correct.

In the story, the word ***showcase*** means ***display***. After Colin showcases, or displays, his skills at kickball, the other kids usually leave him alone because he is a good kickball player.

5. What does it mean that Colin had *a pit in his stomach*?

- (A) He ate too much for breakfast.
- (B) He got motion sickness on the school bus.
- (C) He was starving, and couldn't wait for lunch.
- (D) He was dreading the first day of school.

Hint #1:

Find the part of the story that talks about Colin having a **"pit in his stomach"**.

Hint #2:

When you find the sentence that talks about Colin having a **"pit in his stomach,"** think about the next few sentences following that one, as they explain why he feels the way he does.

Answer: Choice **D** is correct.

The **"pit in his stomach"** is mentioned in the very first line, and the explanation follows. Colin had switched schools a lot and was always getting teased. He was dreading going to school because of the teasing, so choice **D** is the best.

© Kaplan Publishing, Inc.

6. Which of the following is the **best title** for the passage?

(A) Becky and the Bus

(B) The New Kid

(C) How to Play Kickball

(D) Outsmarting Bullies

Hint #1:

Think about the **main idea** of the passage, and then think about the title that most closely matches the main idea.

Hint #2:

Remember, a title should try and capture what the story is mainly about.

Answer: Choice **B** is correct.

The best title for the passage would be: **The New Kid**. The story is mainly about Colin and his first day at school, so a title that refers to Colin is the best choice. All of the other titles have to do with **details** from the story, but not really with the **main idea**.

7. What would Colin **most likely** agree with about being a new kid at a school?

(A) It is fun to be the new kid, because you get all of the attention.

(B) Only new kids who aren't good at sports should be teased.

(C) Being the new kid is no fun, and it's better to stay at the same school.

(D) New kids should never ride the school bus.

Hint #1:

Think about what Colin says about always being the new kid at the beginning of the story.

Hint #2:

Check each answer choice one at a time to see if it's supported by information in the story.

Answer: Choice **C** is correct.

Colin would most likely agree that **being the new kid is no fun, and it's better to stay at the same school.** Colin says that he is going to the fourth school in three years, and wishes that **he could stay long enough to get past the part where the kids teased him every day**. Choice **C** makes the most sense; Colin most likely believes that it's hard to be the new kid and that he would like to be able to stay at the same school.

Read the story, then answer questions 8–11.

Singing Sally and the Giant Water Toad

"AHHHHHHHHHHHHHH!" sang Sally at the top of her lungs. "AAAAAAH! LALALALALALA!"

Sally had on her headphones and was listening to her compact disc player as loud as it could go. She screeched, hummed, and rasped along with her favorite song. Sally didn't have a lot of choices in terms of musical selection, seeing as she lived in the middle of the jungle and all. She had been so lucky to find a CD player containing one, lonely CD, after a group of startled tourists on a jungle tour rushed away from a giant tarantula. Sally knew every sound on that CD, and she loved nothing more than to belt out each number at the top of her lungs, while swinging happily through the trees. Sally didn't really understand what the singer was *saying*, after all, it was in some crazy human language, but Sally knew that she understood what the singer was *feeling*. And wasn't the feeling the most important part?

As Sally chortled and twittered away, members of the group around her looked up from what they were doing, disgusted. It was unheard of for one of her kind to howl so, after all, this was a group of *spider* monkeys, not of horrible, unintelligent *howler* monkeys. As everyone knows, the spiders' brains are more than twice the size of those of the howlers, even if they do technically belong to the same species.

Perhaps most upset of all about Sally's antics was her aunt, Gina. Gina considered herself to be from one of the finest families of all of the spiders, and she just couldn't have her niece squawking away like that, even if she was young and didn't know better. Gina was so embarrassed she could hardly face the rest of the tribe.

On this particular afternoon, Gina had had enough. She marched up to Sally's mother, Annie.

"Listen here, Annie! This noise your dolt of a daughter is making is unacceptable! If you don't make her stop at once, I shall have to ask you to leave our group! I cannot have her hanging around here, *yowling* like a common howler. I have an image to maintain, and maintain it I shall."

"Well hello there, Gina," said Annie patiently. "How nice to see you. Care for a banana, or perhaps some berries?"

"No! All I care for is for you to stop that obnoxious noise coming from that direction!"

Suddenly, there was an ear-splitting sound coming from nearby, and this time, it wasn't Sally. Gina and Annie looked over, only to see a giant horned, green toad rising out of the jungle in the direction of the water hole.

"The Giant Water Toad!" Both Gina and Annie watched in awe, and then both immediately fell to their knees.

Annie whispered, "He's finally come, he's finally come, just like the prophecy proclaimed..."

8. This story is **mainly about**

    (A) the fighting between the spiders and the howlers.

    (B) animals' behavior in the wilderness.

    (D) an ancient prophecy.

    (D) Singing Sally and her family.

Hint #1:

When considering questions about the **main idea**, think about how you would **summarize** the story in one sentence.

Hint #2:

Which of the answer choices is **most similar** to your summary of the story?

Answer: Choice **D** is correct.

This story is mainly about ***Singing Sally and her family***.

Choice **D** is the best because most of the story so far is telling about Sally and her singing, and the problems that this singing is causing in her family.

9. Which of the following **most likely** happened **before** the story took place?

(A) Sally wanted to join the howlers.

(B) Annie heard a prophesy about the Giant Water Toad.

(C) Sally had a dream of singing professionally.

(D) Aunt Gina won a beauty contest.

© Kaplan Publishing, Inc.

Hint #1:

Think about which of the statements can be most easily proven with details from the story.

Hint #2:

Eliminate the choices that have no supporting details in the story.

Answer: Choice **B** is correct.

The only event in the answer choices that must have happened before the story took place is choice **B. Annie must have heard a prophecy about the Giant Water Toad** because she mentions the prophecy in the final two lines. The other events might have occurred, but there are no details in the story that tell us whether they did or did not happen.

10. Why do the spiders think that they are more intelligent than the howlers?

(A) Spiders have brains that are twice as large as the brains of the howlers.

(B) Howlers eat tarantulas.

(C) Howlers are slower than spiders.

(D) The howlers do not believe in the same prophecy as the spiders.

Hint #1:

Go back to the story and read the lines about the howlers' lack of intelligence.

Hint #2:

Check the story for differences between the spiders and the howlers.

Answer: Choice **A** is correct.

At the end of the third paragraph, the story says that **the spiders' brains are more than twice the size of those of the howlers**, which is the reason that the spiders feel they are more intelligent than howlers, so choice **A** is correct.

© Kaplan Publishing, Inc.

11. What is the meaning of the word *yowling* as used in the story?

Ⓐ jumping

Ⓑ teasing

Ⓒ yelling

Ⓓ dancing

Hint #1:

Read the sentence from the passage, replace **yowling** with each word in the answer choices, and think about which one makes the most sense.

Hint #2:

Eliminate the answer choices that do not make sense in the sentence.

Answer: Choice **C** is correct.

As used in the story, **yowling** means **yelling**. Gina says she cannot have Sally **yowling like a common howler**, and because Gina is upset about Sally's singing, we know yowling must be a sound or noise.

Read the passage carefully, then answer questions 12–15.

Once upon a time, there lived a beautiful princess in a grand, faraway palace. She lived with her mother, the queen. When the princess was small, the queen was very busy running the country and didn't have a lot of time to spend with her daughter. To amuse herself, the princess played mostly in the palace garden, throwing rocks into the pond, chasing the swans, and picking flowers.

As the princess grew older, she still spent many an hour in the garden, but her activities of choice began to change. She began to find herself spending nearly all day lying under a great willow tree, daydreaming. She dreamed of being someone different than who she was, someone with a life filled with adventure and excitement. One day, she dreamed she was a great explorer going off to explore uncharted territory. The next day, she dreamed she was an astronaut walking on Mars. Her dreaming didn't stop there. She dreamed she was an acrobat, a professional singer, a writer, a lion tamer, a horse racer, and a juggler.

The princess began to dream about different lives so much that she became very unhappy with her own life. When she wasn't in the garden dreaming, she was moping around the palace, making herself and everyone around her miserable.

One day, she was out in the garden and on this day, she decided to go to a different spot. Instead of sitting under the willow tree, she decided to wander farther away from the castle, toward a patch of tulips. She sat down, and she heard a strange voice. "Hello, princess," said the voice, "I've been waiting for you."

"What? Who are you? Where are you?" the princess shrieked, looking around for the bearer of the voice.

"I am Salamanca, and I am going to grant you your wish of a new destiny."

12. Which of the following **best** describes how the princess is feeling in the **third paragraph**?

- (A) sad
- (B) hopeful
- (C) excited
- (D) angry

Hint #1:

Go back and reread **paragraph three**. Sometimes it helps to refresh your memory about the details of a story!

Hint #2:

Look for words that tell how the princess is feeling.

Answer: Choice **A** is correct.

The princess is probably feeling **sad** in the third paragraph. Rereading paragraph three, we have a great clue to how the princess is feeling in the first sentence; we learn that she became **very unhappy**. A good strategy here after rereading is to look through the answer choices for a **synonym** for **unhappy**, and choice **A**, **sad**, is the best synonym.

13. Which of the following **best** describes how the princess might be feeling at the end of the passage?

(A) depressed

(B) enthusiastic

(C) annoyed

(D) startled

Hint #1:

Go back and reread the **last part** of the passage. Does this give you any clues?

Hint #2:

Think about what happens in the passage and try to imagine how the princess might feel.

Answer: Choice **D** is correct.

At the end of the passage, the princess has just heard a **strange voice** tell her that she is going to change her destiny. The princess shrieks, and then she jumps up and starts asking a lot of questions. Choice **D**, **startled**, makes the most sense.

14. Where do **most** of the important events in the story take place?

(A) The garden

(B) The palace kitchen

(C) The princess's bedroom

(D) A high tower

Hint #1:

Reread the passage and find the most important events. Think about where they all take place.

Hint #2:

Eliminate any places that aren't very important in the story.

Answer: Choice **A** is correct.

This story takes place mostly **in the garden**, because that is where the princess decides that she wants to be something different and that is where she hears the voice, which are the two most important events in the plot.

15. Based on what you read in the story, which of the following will **most likely** happen next?

(A) The princess will slap Salamanca and run away.

(B) A giant frog will appear.

(C) The princess will let Salamanca magically change her into something that she wishes to be.

(D) The story will end.

Hint #1:

Think about what you know about the princess, and about the choice she would probably make when Salamanca appears.

Hint #2:

Eliminate the answer choices that probably won't happen.

Answer: Choice **C** is correct.

Throughout the story, the princess has been thinking about how much she wants to be *someone different*, to change her destiny. It makes the most sense that she **will let Salamanca magically change her into something that she wishes to be**.

Read the poem, then answer questions 16 and 17.

Trees

Beautiful trees sway with the wind

Oh, how I wish I were more like a tree

Swaying and swishing with the wind

But instead I am very stiff

Ready to snap at the smallest sign of change

Trees must know something we don't

About how to make life easy.

16. Why does the author want to be more like a tree?

  (A) Trees are beautiful.

  (B) Trees are not stiff.

  (C) Trees are intelligent.

  (D) Trees change colors.

Hint #1:

Look through the poem for **context clues**.

Hint #2:

How does the author describe himself? How does he describe trees? How are the descriptions different?

Answer: Choice **B** is correct.

The author wants to be more like a tree because **trees are not stiff**.

The author explains in **line 2** that he wishes he were more like a tree because trees sway with the wind and the author is very stiff and ready to snap.

17. Which of the following lines in the poem *Trees* contains **alliteration**?

(A) Line 1

(B) Line 2

(C) Line 4

(D) Line 5

Hint #1:

Alliteration is a poetry device in which a group of words begins with the **same consonant sound**.

Hint #2:

An example of alliteration is: **Martha's marvelous marshmallows**. Because all of the words begin with the **m**- sound, those words really stand out. However, the words **do not** have to be right next to each other!

Answer: Choice **D** is correct.

Line 5 of the poem contains **alliteration** using the **s**- sound, in the phrase **snap at the smallest sign**. This poetry technique emphasizes the words that begin with the letter **s** in the phrase.

Read the following limerick and answer questions 18 and 19.

> There once was a skater named Blake,
>
> Who skated right into a lake.
>
> He grabbed a tree limb,
>
> And screamed, "I can't swim!"
>
> But swears 'twas an honest mistake.

18. What does the word *'twas* mean in **line 5**?

Ⓐ was not

Ⓑ it was

Ⓒ was

Ⓓ is not

Hint #1:

Replace *'twas* with the words in the answer choices and think about which makes the most sense.

Hint #2:

Eliminate the answer choices that do not make sense in the line of the limerick.

Answer: Choice **B** is correct.

The word *'twas* is an old-fashioned **abbreviation** for the words *it was*. Many old poems use this abbreviation, and if you take a look at some of William Shakespeare's writing, you will find this word everywhere!

19. Based on the poem, which of the following describes the **rhyming pattern** of a **limerick**?

(A) AAABA

(B) AABAA

(C) AAABB

(D) AABBA

Hint #1:

When describing the **rhyming pattern** of a poem, the same letter is used for lines that rhyme.

Hint #2:

Look at how the lines of the limerick rhyme. Place the same letter next to the lines that rhyme. Which answer choice matches that rhyming pattern?

Answer: Choice **D** is correct.

In a **limerick**, lines **1**, **2**, and **5** all rhyme, and lines **3** and **4** rhyme. When describing the **rhyming pattern**, each line is represented with a letter, and the same letter is used to represent lines that rhyme. Line **1** is first, so it's represented with the letter **A**, and so are lines **2** and **5** because they all rhyme. Lines **3** and **4** rhyme with each other, so they are represented with the letter **B**. This chart might help to clear things up a bit:

Line 1: A

Line 2: A

Line 3: B

Line 4: B

Line 5: A

Choice **D** matches this **rhyming pattern**.

Challenge Activity

You're doing a great job so far!
Are you ready for a Challenge Activity?
Good luck!

The following story is a bit longer and a bit more complex than the others. Do your best to read through it carefully, pausing as you read to think about the characters and what is happening.

The Wolf and the Girl

"I'll never find any food for my family," grumbled the wolf to himself. "It's been such a long, tedious winter, and my children are starving. There must be someone around who can give me some food." He had stopped to rest in a small clearing. He scratched his back on a fallen tree branch, and then continued on in his task of searching for food in the deep of the forest. He had resorted to collecting nuts and tree berries so as not to starve to death months ago, and because he and his family liked the taste and the availability of the food, they decided to become vegetarians. However, the wolf didn't like to do the collecting himself. He waited until he saw a smaller animal collecting food, then he jumped out and scared it, and took all of the food it had worked so hard to collect.

Just then, the wolf heard a tiny voice coming from the other side of the clearing. For a while, the wolf couldn't see the body that belonged to the voice, when, all of a sudden, a bright red cloak popped into view.

"What a lovely day to visit grandmother, *tra, la, la…*" sang the voice. The wolf's eyes focused on a young girl, not much taller than he was himself, wearing a deep red riding cloak.

The cloak was too big, and the hood nearly covered the girl's face and made her trip as she walked. The wolf also noticed that the girl was carrying a large basket of something that smelled wonderful. It smelled like some kind of sweet zucchini bread or maybe corn muffins. Whatever it was, the wolf knew he wanted some.

"Hello, young lady," said the wolf, sauntering out to meet the girl. "I mean, *Grr!*"

"AHHHH! A wolf!" screamed the girl. "My grandmother told me if I saw one of you, I was to hit you with this!"

With that, she pulled a thick piece of wood out of her bag, with which she promptly and repeatedly tried to hit the wolf over the head.

"Stop it!" cried the wolf. "You're supposed to be scared of me, silly girl! You're supposed to drop your basket and run away!"

"Hmm," said the girl, appearing to consider what the wolf was saying. "Well, I guess you can have one of my muffins. I have a special one that I think you would like."

"Thanks!" said the wolf, grabbing the muffin and gulping it down. Right away, he began to feel very sleepy. His eyelids felt very heavy, and he couldn't seem to hold his head up anymore. He thought about asking the girl for another muffin, but before he had the chance, he fell right into a very deep sleep.

"Ha-ha!" laughed the girl, "Mom was right, I'm glad I brought along some instant-sleep muffins! I brought them to help Grandma to get some rest, but now that wolf won't be bothering me anymore!" And with that, she skipped off to her Grandmother's house.

The wolf didn't wake up for many hours, and when he did, it took him a few minutes to remember what had happened. "Well, I've learned my lesson," thought the wolf. "Never talk to strangers in the forest, even if the stranger is a cute little girl with a basket full of delicious-smelling goodies. From now on, I'm going to do all of the food collecting myself." After a while, the wolf's wife came and found him, and together they set off in search of berries.

Answer the following questions about the passage. These questions have a different format from questions you've answered before in this workbook; they ask to you write answers instead of choosing an answer from a list.

a) Who are the **main characters** in the story?

_____

_____

_____

_____

b) How does the girl trick the wolf?

_____

_____

_____

_____

c) What is the lesson that the wolf learns at the end?

_____

_____

_____

_____

Answers to Challenge Activity:

Your answers may look a little different than these, but as long as they have the same main ideas, you're doing great!

a) The main characters are the wolf and the girl. The wolf's wife comes in at the end of the story, but she isn't really a main character because she is only in a small part of the story.

b) The girl gives the wolf a muffin, and he thinks she is just being nice and giving him a delicious snack. But the muffin that she gives him has something in it that makes him fall asleep.

c) The wolf learns that it's safer to collect all of his own food. He had been bullying smaller animals into giving him some of their food, but because this plan doesn't work so well with the girl, he decides to collect the food himself.

Let's take a quick test and see how much you've learned during this climb up *SCORE!* Mountain.

Good luck!

Read the following story, then answer the questions that follow.

Maria was very excited for her trip. She was going to take a train across the country to California, where her cousins lived. She had been asking her dad questions about the trip for weeks.

"Will we really sleep on the train?"

"Yes, Maria, there are special cars on the train called sleeper cars. They have beds in them that fold out where we can sleep," answered her father.

Maria also wondered what they would eat on the train. "What will we eat on the train, Dad?"

"There is a dining car, which is almost like a restaurant. We can eat there."

Finally, the day arrived for the trip. Maria had packed very carefully after asking her father many questions about what to bring. She couldn't wait to get on the train!

When they got to the train station, there was a long wait because the train was delayed.

"How long do we have to wait, Dad?"

"About two hours," he answered.

Maria felt very impatient. Finally, the train arrived, and Maria jumped on excitedly with her father right behind her. The conductor rang the bell to signal that the train was leaving, and *whoosh!* off they went.

Maria looked out the window, wondering what surprises the trip would bring.

1. Who is Maria going to visit on her trip?

    Ⓐ her father
    Ⓑ her father's friend
    Ⓒ her cousins
    Ⓓ her grandparents

2. Why does Maria feel impatient in the story?

    Ⓐ She is waiting for the train to be cleaned.
    Ⓑ She wants to see her cousins.
    Ⓒ Her dad won't answer all of her questions.
    Ⓓ The train is delayed.

3. Which of the following is the best title for the story?

    Ⓐ Maria's First Train Trip
    Ⓑ Maria's Summer Vacation
    Ⓒ Maria and Her Father
    Ⓓ Maria Visits Her Cousins

4. Which best describes Maria's feeling about going on the train trip?

(A) worried

(B) thrilled

(C) angry

(D) impatient

5. Which of the following **best describes** the mood at the end of the story?

(A) hopeful

(B) scary

(C) rushed

(D) surprising

Answers to test questions:

1. Choice **C** is correct.
You can find the answer to this question in the second sentence: **She was going to take a train across the country to California, where her cousins lived**. Remember to go back and check the passage when answering questions that ask you about a **detail** from the passage.

2. Choice **D** is correct.
The passage explains that Maria is impatient because there is a long wait for the train at the station because **the train is delayed**.

3. Choice **A** is correct.
The best title for this story, the one that best describes the story as a whole, is: **Maria's First Train Trip**.

4. Choice **B** is correct.
The first sentence tells us that Maria is excited about her trip. The best synonym for excited is choice **B**, **thrilled**.

5. Choice **A** is correct.
The **mood** of a story is part of the story's setting. Creating the mood of a story is an important part of helping the reader to understand the story. In general, this story has a happy feeling, and at the end, Maria is wondering what surprises the trip will bring. The best way to describe the mood is **hopeful**, because she is happy and excited about the trip ahead.

Celebrate!

Let's take a fun break before we go to the next base camp. You've earned it!

Let's start a **journal**!

You will need:

- Some paper or a blank notebook

- A pen or pencil

You can write about whatever you like in your journal!

Use your journal to keep your private thoughts, your goals and dreams, stories, and fond memories. It's up to you!

Decorate your journal any way you like. Let it express who you are!

Congratulations!
You're almost to the top of _SCORE!_ Mountain.

The rest is up to you! Try to set aside some time each day to write in your journal.

Write about whatever you like!

Keeping a journal is a great way to express yourself and improve your writing skills!

Good luck and have fun!
You deserve it for working so hard!

Base Camp

6

Everyday Writing

You've made it to the final base camp! Outstanding! Make it through and you'll be at the top of *SCORE!* Mountain. You can do it! Good luck!

SCORE! MOUNTAIN TOP

BASE CAMP 5

BASE CAMP 4

BASE CAMP 3

BASE CAMP 2

BASE CAMP 1

Read the passage below, then answer questions 1–3.

Writing is used in our lives in many different ways. For example, people use it to entertain each other with stories. People also use writing to help others to understand where to go, as in directions and signs, as well as to provide information, as in newspapers.

There are several techniques that good writers use as they write. Some of them are listed below. Perhaps you've used them before. They're part of the *Writing Process*, and you can use it to write anything from a letter to a friend to a five-paragraph essay.

Here are the steps:

The Writing Process

Step 1: Brainstorming—thinking about and gathering ideas for what to write.

Step 2: Researching—gathering information about whom or what you are writing about.

Step 3: Writing—writing down all of your ideas.

Step 4: Revising—looking over your writing to make sure it is just the way you want it.

Step 5: Proofreading—fixing any mistakes in your writing, including grammar and facts, to make sure that your writing is as correct as possible.

1. You are writing an article about the signing of the Declaration of Independence and while looking it over for mistakes, you realized you have written the wrong year. You correct your error. Which step in the writing process is this?

(A) Step 1

(B) Step 3

(C) Step 4

(D) Step 5

Hint #1:

Review the steps of the writing process.

Hint #2:

During which step do you correct your mistakes?

Answer: Choice **D** is correct.

During the **proofreading** stage, you fix any mistakes in your writing, including grammar and facts, to make sure that your writing is as correct as possible.

2. You are writing a report about spiders, and you want to learn more about their eating and sleeping habits. You search a website about spiders on the Internet for some facts.

Which step in the writing process is this?

(A) Step 2

(B) Step 5

(C) Step 1

(D) Step 4

Hint #1:

Carefully review the steps of the writing process.

Hint #2:

During which step would you **gather information** about spiders?

Answer: Choice **A** is correct.

During the **researching stage**, you gather information about whom or what you are writing about.

3. Your English teacher tells the class about a new assignment. She says that each student will choose his or her favorite book and write a report that includes a summary and review of the book. You decide to go to the library after school and find a book you would like to write about.

Which step in the writing process is this?

(A) Step 2

(B) Step 1

(C) Step 3

(D) Step 4

Hint #1:

Do you remember which step of the writing process this is?

Hint #2:

During which step would you **think about** what you want to write about?

Answer: Choice **B** is correct.

During the **brainstorming stage**, you think about and gather ideas for what to write.

© Kaplan Publishing, Inc.

4. Joanna is writing a short story for her creative writing class. She is trying to come up with a synonym for the word *good*, to make her writing more interesting.

Where is the **best** place for Joanna to research possible synonyms?

(A) a book of short stories

(B) a thesaurus

(C) a magazine

(D) a newspaper

Hint #1:

Have you used the items in the answer choices before? How have you used them?

Hint #2:

What is a good source for information about different words?

Answer: Choice **B** is correct.

A **thesaurus** is a resource that contains synonyms of various words. If you are using the same word over and over again in your writing, it's a good idea to use a thesaurus to come up with some new words that have the same meaning, to prevent your work from becoming boring or repetitious. It makes your writing more interesting!

5. Clarence is proofreading a report he had written on the solar system. He wants to make sure that his report has the correct spelling of the planet Mercury.

What is the **best** resource for Clarence to use?

(A) A telescope

(B) A science-fiction novel

(C) A dictionary

(D) A thesaurus

Hint #1:

Have you used the items in the answer choices before? How have you used them?

Hint #2:

Eliminate any answer choices that don't give you information about different words.

Answer: Choice **C** is correct.

A **dictionary** is a good resource to check your spelling. Using proper spelling is an essential part of good writing!

6. Jonelle wants to write an article for her school newspaper on delicious study break snacks that kids can make. She is at the library, brainstorming ideas for her article.

What would be the **best** place for Jonelle to look to help her come up with ideas?

Ⓐ a cooking website on the Internet for good recipes

Ⓑ a dictionary for the meaning of the word delicious

Ⓒ a local phone book for pizza restaurants that deliver

Ⓓ what the librarian is eating for lunch

Hint:

Imagine that **you** are writing this article for your school newspaper. Where would you look for ideas?

Answer: Choice **A** is correct.

Jonelle is writing an article for her school newspaper on delicious study-break snacks that kids can make. She should look for snack recipes that kids can make. The best place to look for such recipes would be on **a cooking website on the Internet**.

Read the following article from a local school newspaper and the paragraph that follows, then answer questions 7–11.

Yesterday was a very unusual Monday for Mr. Harrison's fifth-grade class at Lincoln Elementary School. The students were very surprised when their teacher, Mr. Harrison, told them that they would not be getting any homework. The students had no idea why Mr. Harrison made this very strange decision. Mr. Harrison did not explain himself, he simply told them to take the night off and rest.

At the end of the day, when Mr. Harrison usually asks the students to take out their assignment notebooks to write down their homework assignments, he told the students that they would not have any assignments. Many of the students really wanted to find out the reason that they were not given homework. But Mr. Harrison refused to tell them. He only said something about a surprise coming up, and that they needed to be well rested.

Yesterday was the first Monday all year that the students in grade five did not receive homework. Usually on Mondays, students get about two to three hours of homework. The students seem to have been getting more work each week, so it came as a real surprise that they didn't have any homework at all.

For some students, such as Jackie Thomas, the surprise of having no homework was almost ruined because Mr. Harrison would not announce the reason. "I just wish he would tell us!" said Jackie. "I'm worried that it's because we have a ton more work coming up next week." For other students, such as Don Ford, the surprise was not ruined at all. Don said, "I don't care why we don't have homework, I'm going to have fun tonight!" Mr. Harrison said that the students would find out next week why they didn't have homework, and that they shouldn't worry too much.

–By Lily Matthewson

A very important part of newspaper articles are the **five *Ws***
and one *H*: *who?*, *what?*, *when?*, *where?*, *why?*, and *how?*
When writing a newspaper article, you should make sure that
your story talks about all of these.

7. **Who** is the article about?

_____

_____

_____

_____

Hint:

Carefully review the article for
who it is about.

Answer: The article is about **Mr. Harrison's fifth-grade class**.

8. Where do the events in the article take place?

_____

_____

_____

_____

Hint:

The article tells you **where** the events in the story take place. Can you find it?

Answer: The article takes place at **Lincoln Elementary School.**

9. When did the events in the article happen?

_____

_____

_____

_____

Hint:

Lily Matthewson tells you **when** the events in the story took place. Can you find it?

Answer: According to the article, the events took place **yesterday**, which was a Monday.

10. What happened in the article?

_____

_____

_____

_____

Hint:

Carefully review the article and try to **summarize** the events in a sentence or two.

Answer: Your retelling of the events in the article may be slightly different from this one, but if the basic facts are the same, then you're on the right track:

The students in Mr. Harrison's fifth-grade class were surprised yesterday when they didn't get any homework. Mr. Harrison said that the students would find out next week why they didn't have homework.

11. Which of the following is the **best title** for the article?

(A) I Love My School!

(B) What's Your Favorite Subject?

(C) All about Mr. Harrison

(D) Students Surprised!

Hint #1:

A title should give a good idea as to what the article is about.

Hint #2:

Eliminate any answer choices that do not have anything to do with what the article is about.

Answer: Choice **D** is correct.

The best title for the article is **Students Surprised!** Remember, the article is mainly about how the students in Mr. Harrison's fifth-grade class were surprised yesterday when they didn't get any homework. Choice **D** best captures what the article is about.

12. Imagine you are a reporter, writing a newspaper article about the new lunches being served in your school cafeteria.

Which of the following techniques would be **least** helpful for your article?

(A) Interview students about what they think of the new lunches being served.

(B) Bring your lunch from home while writing your article.

(C) Gather a list of the new lunches that are being served and try them for yourself.

(D) Interview the school principal and ask why there are new lunches being served.

Hint #1:

Read the question carefully. Remember, you are looking for the least helpful technique.

Hint #2:

Which of the techniques in the answer choices would help you collect the least amount of information on the new lunches being served in your school cafeteria?

Answer: Choice **B** is correct.

Remember, you're writing a newspaper article about the new lunches being served in your school cafeteria. **Bringing your lunch from home** wouldn't be very helpful when writing the article, would it?

Read the information below and answer questions 13–15.

Movie reviews are a helpful way for people to figure out which movies they would like to see. Like newspaper articles, movie reviews often have a specific format.

Here's a basic outline for a typical movie review.

1. **Title:** Name of movie

2. **Reviewed by:** Your name

3. **General Information:** A bulleted list of the director, the main actors, and the rating

4. **Summary Paragraph:** Answer the first four W questions: who?, what?, when?, and where? (This will give the reader a good overview of the movie.)

5. **Opinion Paragraph:** Answer the last two questions, how? and why? (This will give the reader your opinion about the movie. You can also include other people's opinions using quotes if you have them.)

13. In which part of a movie review would you find the following sentence?

> "This was a horrible movie! It was boring, slow, and a total waste of time. Do yourself a favor and see something else!"

Ⓐ Reviewed by

Ⓑ General information

Ⓒ Summary paragraph

Ⓓ Opinion paragraph

Hint #1:

Review the basic outline of a typical movie review.

Hint #2:

Does the sentence sound like facts about a movie?

Answer: Choice **D** is correct.

You would find this sentence in the **opinion paragraph** of a movie review. It's a pretty strong opinion, isn't it?

14. Tyler is writing a very positive review of a great new movie he has just seen. He is very proud of his work, and now just needs to sign his name to it. In which part of a movie review is the **signature** usually found?

(A) the title section

(B) the reviewed by section

(C) the general information section

(D) the summary paragraph

Hint #1:

Where's the right place to let people know who wrote the movie review?

Hint #2:

Eliminate the answer choices that you know the signature doesn't belong in.

Answer: Choice **B** is correct.

The movie reviewer's signature is usually found in ***the reviewed by section***.

15. Try and unscramble the parts of the following movie review so it follows the basic outline for a typical review.

(1) *Ollie* is a movie about three friends who magically become expert skateboarders overnight.

(2) Directed by: Bernie Bales
Lead Actors: Joshua Sam, Eugene Nichols, and Frankie Fill
Rated: G

(3) "This is one of the best movies of the year," said Sarah Brendt, a sixth grader, as she left the movie theater.

(4) *Ollie*

(5) At the end of the movie, the friends realize that magic isn't the best way to learn to skateboard after all.

Which of the following is the **correct order** for the parts of the movie review?

Ⓐ 1, 2, 3, 4, 5

Ⓑ 4, 2, 3, 1, 5

Ⓒ 4, 2, 1, 3, 5

Ⓓ 4, 2, 1, 5, 3

Hint #1:

Be sure to refer to the basic outline for a movie review!

Hint #2:

Remember, an opinion is a personal view or belief that cannot be proven.

Answer: Choice **D** is the correct order.
The first line should be the title, so **part 4** must be first. Next is the general information, which we have in **part 2**. The next part in the review is the summary, and **part 1** and **part 5** are both part of the summary. So, which should come **first**? **Part 1** should, because it is about the beginning of the movie, and **part 5** is about the end. And finally, **part 3** should come last, because it is part of the opinion paragraph.

16. Michelle's good friend Heather moved to a new town last summer, and Michelle wants to write to her to see how she is doing. She needs help with the **format** of writing a letter to a friend.

Michelle should look at a sample **formal letter** as a guide when writing her letter to Heather.

True   False

Hint #1:

When do you write a formal letter?

Hint #2:

When do you write a friendly letter?

Answer: False

Michelle should look at a sample **friendly letter**. A **friendly letter** is a letter you would write to someone you know, such as a good friend or family member.

The following friendly letter contains a few mistakes. Read the letter, then answer the questions.

17. Which of the following parts of the letter contains a **format mistake**?

(A) 1
(B) 2
(C) 3
(D) 4

1
16 East Flatbush Dr.
Brooklyn, NY 10012

July 28, 2005

2
Dear Simon,
　How are you? How are things in New York? I heard that it is very hot there, like it's some kind of record. Be sure that you drink lots of water, and that you don't go out in the middle of the day. I'm glad the pool!

3
　We missed you at camp this year, but we had a great time. We went canoeing, rafting, and on an overnight camping trip. We even got to see some bear cubs, which was pretty cool. I was glad the mother didn't come out!

　Well, hope things are good with you, and I hope you hear from you soon.

4
Your friend,
Alex

5

6

Hint #1:

A **format mistake** simply means a mistake in how the letter should look when compared to the standard format.

Hint #2:

How does this letter differ from a standard friendly letter?

Answer: Choice **B** is correct.

The format mistake is in **part 2**. Alex should **skip a line** after the greeting.

18. Celia just got a new computer and was eager to set it up and use it. Unfortunately, when she opened the box, it seemed to be missing an important piece. She would like to write a **letter** to the company and ask for the missing piece so that she can finish setting up her new computer.

Celia is not sure what type of letter she should write. Can you help her?

Celia should write a _____ letter.

Hint #1:

What type of letter do you write to companies and organizations?

Hint #2:

In what situations should you write a friendly letter?

© Kaplan Publishing, Inc.

Answer: Celia should write a **business letter**.

People write **business letters** mainly to companies and organizations, and they are a bit more formal than a friendly letter. The format of a business letter is also slightly different from the format of a friendly letter.

Let's take a look at a sample business letter. The following letter contains a few mistakes. Read the letter, then answer the question.

19. Which of the following parts of the letter contains a **format mistake**?

Ⓐ 1

Ⓑ 2

Ⓒ 3

Ⓓ 4

1 ⌈ 16 East Flatbush Dr.
Brooklyn, NY 10012

2 ⌈ July 28, 2005

3 ⌈ Marjorie Lewis
Camp Director
Camp Bear Claw
776 Little Rock Road
Westville, NH 40993

Dear Ms. Lewis,

4 ⌈   I am writing this letter to let you know that I would like to apply for a job as a camp counselor at your camp. I have been a camper at your camp for ten years, and I really enjoy spending time there.

5 ⌈ Your camp is beautiful, and I know all about the campgrounds and the activities you offer, two reasons that I would make a good counselor. I really hope you consider Me for the job

 If you have any questions, please let me know. I would love to talk to you soon about the job. I will call you to set up a time to talk.

Sincerely
Alex P. Gregory

6 ⌊

Hint:

Think about ways that the format of a **business letter** is different from the format of a **friendly letter**.

Answer: Choice **D** is correct.

Alex should not have **indented** the first paragraph because this is a **business letter**. Business letters have what are called **block paragraphs**, which aren't indented. In general, though, Alex's format is pretty good!

Challenge Activity

You're doing a great job so far!
Are you ready for a Challenge Activity?
Good luck!

Read the information below and test your writing skills with a different kind of challenge: writing your own story!

Here are the four essential parts of a story:

1. **Exposition (beginning):** The exposition is a fancy word for the beginning of the story. This is the part in which the author introduces the characters and describes the setting.

2. **Plot Build-Up:** During this part of the story, most of the action happens. During this part, the excitement builds and the plot gets more complicated.

3. **Climax:** This is the most exciting part of the story. This is the part where the characters face their final challenge, or finally get where they were trying to go. This is the part of the story where, when you get to it while you are reading, it's hard to put down the book.

4. **Dénouement (ending):** The dénouement is a fancy word for the ending of the story, where everything gets wrapped up and all of the questions are answered.

Remember the steps of the writing process: **brainstorming, researching, writing, revising,** and **proofreading.** They are the keys to making your writing as good as it can be!

The next part is up to you. Get a few blank sheets of paper, follow the steps above, and write your story!

Answers to Challenge Activity:
Everyone's story will be different, so answers will vary. When you are
finished writing your story, have a parent, guardian or teacher read it, and
ask for feedback. Having someone else read your work is very helpful. Even
the best authors in the world have many people check their work!

Let's take a quick test and see how much you've learned during this climb up *SCORE!* Mountain.

Good luck!

1. Which of the following is not an element of the writing process?

   (A) brainstorming

   (B) researching

   (C) waiting

   (D) revising

2. Which of the following parts of a newspaper article belongs in the lead paragraph, which answers the five *Ws* and one *H* questions?

   (A) Before the game, the Titans had been training four days a week.

   (B) Terrific Titans Do it Again

   (C) By Jane Hanson

   (D) Last night, the Tannisberg Titans won the series for the second time in a row.

3. Which of the following parts of a movie review belongs in the opinion paragraph?

Ⓐ Reviewed by Sasha Bardsley

Ⓑ *Moonlight Patrol* is the story of security guards who see an alien spaceship.

Ⓒ "I didn't understand the movie at all, so I was kind of bored," said one moviegoer.

Ⓓ The plot is a bit confusing, because at the beginning of the movie many things happen at the same time.

4. The following movie review is scrambled! Read the parts, and then choose the best order.

a. Reviewed by Mimi LaCroix

b. Personally, I felt that this movie was a bit dull.

c. I found it dull because none of the action really happened until near the end of the movie.

d. Harry Hundouli, the main character, finds himself trapped underwater in a tiny castle.

e. Harry and the Underwater Castle

Ⓐ e, a, d, b, c

Ⓑ e, d, b, c, a

Ⓒ a, e, d, b, c

Ⓓ e, a, b, c, d

5. The following business letter is scrambled!
Read the parts and then choose the best order.

1.   May 14, 2005

2.   Mrs. Edwina Crumpnick
    Director of Customer Service
    Nifty Nuts, Incorporated
    66790 Salamander Place
    Roebuck, MI 34993

3.   Sincerely yours,

4.   I am writing this letter to tell you that I purchased a
    terrible bag of nuts from your company.

5.   45 Great Goose Lane
    Jack-o-lantern Drive
    Roebuck, MI 34993

(A) 1, 2, 5, 4, 3

(B) 5, 1, 2, 4, 3

(C) 2, 1, 5, 4, 3

(D) 5, 1, 2, 3, 4

Answers to test questions:

1. Choice **C** is correct.

   Remember the steps of the writing process: **brainstorming**, **researching**, **writing**, **revising**, and **proofreading**. Remember, they are the keys to making your writing as good as it can be!

2. Choice **D** is correct.

   Many people only read the first paragraph of newspaper articles because this paragraph gives most of the important information. Choice **D** tells us **who** the article is about, and also tells us **what** happened, so it would definitely belong in the lead paragraph.

3. Choice **C** is correct.

   This quote is an **opinion**, so it would certainly belong in the opinion paragraph.

4. Choice **A** is correct.

   The **title** of the movie should come first, so **part e** should be first. Then, the **reviewe**r should come next, which is **part a**. Now, looking at the remaining parts, **parts b** and **c** belong in the **opinion paragraph**, and **part d** belongs in the **summary paragraph**, so part **d** must come first.

5. Choice **B** is correct.

   The first part of a business letter is the **heading**, which contains the return address and the date. **Part 5** is the **return address** because it doesn't have a name that goes with it, and **part 1** is, of course, the **date**. The next part of a business letter is the **inside address**. **Part 2** is the **inside address**, so that comes next. **Part 4** belongs in the **body** of the letter, and it should come before **part 3**, because **part 3** is in the **closing**.

Celebrate!

You did a great job! Let's have some fun and celebrate your success! You've earned it!

Go outside, get some fresh air, and visit a friend!

You deserve a fun break from studying.

Go visit a good friend and have some fun!

Try spending some time with your friend doing something fun!

Congratulations!
You've made it to the top of *SCORE!* Mountain.

Maybe you'd like to see a movie?

Maybe you like video games?

Maybe you like playing sports?

The choice is yours!

You've worked hard! Now it's time to have some fun!
You've earned it!

Have a great time!

You should be really proud! I knew you could make it to the top!

Here are some helpful tools to guide you through each base camp!

Use these tools whenever you need a helpful hand during your climb up _SCORE!_ Mountain.

Here is a chart of common word roots and their meanings:

Root	Definition	Example
circum-	around	circumference
pend-	hanging	pending
mar-	having to do with the ocean	marina
terra-	land	extraterrestrial
frac-	a piece	fracture
geo-	earth	geography
bio-	life	biology
micro-	small	microscope

Here is a chart of common suffixes and their meanings:

Suffix	Definition	Example
-less	without	boneless
-ist	one who does something	saxophonist
-er	one who does something	reviewer
-ee	one who is	employee
-ish	like	childish
-ology	study of	biology

Here is a chart of common prefixes and their meanings:

Prefix	Definition	Example
re-	again	rewrite
un-	not	unable
mis-	wrong	misspelling
il-	not	illiterate
pre-	before	preassemble
extra-	beyond	extracurricular
ex-	out	exhale

synonym: a word that is the same in meaning or is close in meaning to a given word. Example: *close* and *near*.

antonym: a word that is the opposite or nearly the opposite of a given word. Example: *love* and *hate*.

homonym: a word that is spelled the same as a given word but has a different meaning. Example: *fall* (the action verb) and *fall* (the season).

homophone: a word that sounds the same as a given word, but is spelled differently and has a different meaning. Example: *hare* and *hair*.

The 5 Steps of the Writing Process

Step 1: Brainstorming—thinking about and gathering ideas for what to write.

Step 2: Researching—gathering information about whom or what you are writing about.

Step 3: Writing—writing down all of your ideas.

Step 4: Revising—looking over your writing to make sure it is just the way you want it.

Step 5: Proofreading—fixing any mistakes in your writing, including grammar and facts, to make sure that your writing is as correct as possible.

The 4 Essential Parts of a Story

Step 1: Exposition (Beginning)—the beginning of the story. This is the part in which the author introduces the characters and describes the setting.

Step 2: Plot Build-Up—during this part of the story, most of the action happens. During this part, the excitement builds and the plot gets more complicated.

Step 3: Climax—this is the most exciting part of the story. This is the part where the characters face their final challenge, or finally get where they were trying to go. This is the part of the story where, when you get to it while you are reading, it's hard to put down the book.

Step 4: Dénouement (Ending)—the ending of the story, where everything gets wrapped up, and all of the questions are answered.

You can do it!

Use these blank pages to work out the questions in your
SCORE! Mountain Challenge Workbook.

You can do it!

You can do it!

You can do it!

You can do it!